Social Issues
in Literature

Coming of Age in
Sue Monk Kidd's
The Secret Life of Bees

Other Books in the Social Issues in Literature Series:

Social Issues
in Literature

Coming of Age in
Sue Monk Kidd's
The Secret Life of Bees

Dedria Bryfonski, Book Editor

GREENHAVEN PRESS
A part of Gale, Cengage Learning

Detroit • New York • San Francisco • New Haven, Conn • Waterville, Maine • London

Elizabeth Des Chenes, *Director, Publishing Solutions*

© 2013 Greenhaven Press, a part of Gale, Cengage Learning

Gale and Greenhaven Press are registered trademarks used herein under license.

For more information, contact:
Greenhaven Press
27500 Drake Rd.
Farmington Hills, MI 48331-3535
Or you can visit our Internet site at gale.cengage.com

For product information and technology assistance, contact us at

Gale Customer Support, 1-800-877-4253
For permission to use material from this text or product, submit all requests online at www.cengage.com/permissions

Further permissions questions can be emailed to permissionrequest@cengage.com

Articles in Greenhaven Press anthologies are often edited for length to meet page requirements. In addition, original titles of these works are changed to clearly present the main thesis and to explicitly indicate the author's opinion. Every effort is made to ensure that Greenhaven Press accurately reflects the original intent of the authors. Every effort has been made to trace the owners of copyrighted material.

Cover image © John Krondes/ZUMA Wire Service/Alamy.

LIBRARY OF CONGRESS CATALOGING-IN-PUBLICATION DATA

Coming of Age in Sue Monk Kidd's The Secret Life of Bees / Dedria Bryfonski, Book Editor.
pages cm. -- (Social Issues in Literature)
Includes bibliographical references and index.
ISBN 978-0-7377-6383-6 (hardcover) -- ISBN 978-0-7377-6384-3 (pbk.)
1. Kidd, Sue Monk. Secret life of bees. 2. Bildungsromans, American--History and criticism. 3. Christian fiction, American--History and criticism. 4. Bryfonski, Dedria, editor of compilation.
PS3611.I44S3826 2013
813'.6--dc23
2012040866

Printed in Mexico
2 3 4 5 6 7 17 16 15 14 13

Contents

Women in the American South typically had limited roles open to them. Lily, without a mother or a female role model, finds the Daughters of Mary, who connect her to the Black Madonna. Lily undergoes a transformation as she releases the spiritual power within herself.

Chapter 3: Contemporary Perspectives on Coming of Age

Adults can have any one or more of a variety of problems that make them poor parents. Sometimes those problems are obvious, such as abusing substances, and sometimes problems are less obvious, such as not taking into account a child's real feelings.

Introduction

In telling the story of Lily Owens, the motherless teenager who grows to emotional and spiritual maturity in the pages of *The Secret Life of Bees*, Sue Monk Kidd employs the coming-of-age genre, a genre based on the German *bildungsroman*. Although the first *bildungsroman*, or formation novel, was most likely *The History of Agathon*, written by Christoph Martin Wieland in 1766–1767, Johann Wolfgang von Goethe's *Wilhelm Meister's Apprenticeship*, written in 1795–1796, is the most famous early example of the genre. In 1819 philologist Karl Morgenstern coined the term *bildungsroman* in his lectures at the University of Dorpat. During the course of a *bildungsroman*, the protagonist grows from youth to maturity. Typically the young person embarks on a journey—usually leaving home—undergoes a crisis and is tested, and emerges as an emotionally mature adult.

As the genre migrated to the United States, the *bildungsroman* became known as the coming-of-age novel. One of the earliest American coming-of-age novels is also one of the most famous—Mark Twain's *The Adventures of Huckleberry Finn*, published in 1885. Other well-known examples of American coming-of-age novels are Harper Lee's *To Kill a Mockingbird*, John Knowles's *A Separate Peace*, and J.D. Salinger's *The Catcher in the Rye*. According to critic Kenneth Millard, the coming-of-age novel is particularly well suited as a vehicle for exploring American culture and national identity because a belief in constant renewal, regeneration, and self-invention is such a strong part of the American ethos. The coming-of-age novel shares many similarities with the *bildungsroman*: the protagonist is a young person who is at odds with society, faces a series of trials and tribulations, and emerges from these experiences as an emotionally mature adult. However, there is one important difference between the

American coming-of-age novel and the *bildungsroman*: in the German form, the protagonist is always a young man; in the American form the main character can be of either gender.

The Secret Life of Bees is a classic coming-of-age story. The protagonist, Lily Owens, is not simply motherless, but is also guilty of accidentally killing her mother. Her father is emotionally distant and abusive, and her sole companion is her black housekeeper, Rosaleen. As the novel begins, the young, white Lily is self-absorbed, ignorant of the racial tensions dividing the South, and haunted by the fear that her mother deserted her. Lily and Rosaleen escape their hometown after Rosaleen is arrested for defying white racists when registering to vote. Their journey takes them to the home of the three beekeeping Boatwright sisters, black women who are part of the Daughters of Mary religious group. Over the course of the summer, Lily learns that her mother did not intend to desert her, and she comes to accept her role in her mother's death. She also comes to a more enlightened view of race relations in the South. And, most importantly, Lily experiences a spiritual awakening that allows her to discover the nurturing presence of the Black Madonna in herself. Kidd emphasizes the centrality of the theme of spiritual growth on her website, suemonk kidd.com:

> As I began *[The Secret Life of Bees]*, I wanted the driving impetus in Lily's life to be the search for home and for her mother. But clearly in the back of my mind, I knew there was a less tangible, more symbolic search for home and mother that needed to take place: a coming *home* to herself and the discovery of the mother within. I knew Lily would have to find an undreamed of strength, and that she would do it the same way the powerful black women around her did it—through the empowerment of a divine feminine presence, in this case a Black Mary.
>
> I felt that any image of Mary in the novel would have to be black. Not only because the women who revered her were

black, but because historically Black Madonnas have often been at the root of insurgence. . . . I decided I would create a Black Madonna for the novel, who had existed during slavery in the South, and that she would be a symbol of freedom and consolation.

The Secret Life of Bees quickly became a best-selling novel and one frequently taught in schools. In Chapters 1 and 2 of this *Social Issues in Literature* volume, reviewers and literary critics discuss the theme of coming of age in Monk's first novel. Chapter 3 presents contemporary perspectives on the topic of coming of age.

Chronology

1948

Kidd is born August 12 in Albany, Georgia.

1970

Kidd receives her BS in nursing from Texas Christian University.

1987

God's Joyful Surprise: Finding Yourself Loved is published.

1988

All Things Are Possible is published.

1990

When the Heart Waits: Spiritual Direction for Life's Sacred Questions and *Love's Hidden Blessings: God Can Touch Your Life When You Least Expect It* are published.

1996

The Dance of the Dissident Daughter: A Woman's Journey from Christian Tradition to the Sacred Feminine is published.

2002

The Secret Life of Bees is published.

2005

The Mermaid Chair and *A Luminous Presence: One Woman's Awakening to the Inner Life* are published.

2006

Firstlight: The Early Inspirational Writings of Sue Monk Kidd is published.

2008

The movie version of *The Secret Life of Bees* is released.

2009

Traveling with Pomegranates: A Mother-Daughter Story, written by Monk with her daughter, Ann Kidd Taylor, is published.

Social Issues
in Literature

CHAPTER 1

Background on
Sue Monk Kidd

The Life of Sue Monk Kidd

Contemporary Literary Criticism

Contemporary Literary Criticism *is an ongoing multivolume series that contains critical essays on contemporary novelists, dramatists, poets, short story writers, and other creative writers.*

Sue Monk Kidd has been a writer for most of her life, according to the editors of Contemporary Literary Criticism. *As a child she wrote narratives based on the stories told by her father. In her twenties, she became interested in spirituality, particularly the works of American Catholic monk and writer Thomas Merton, and she began writing articles and books addressing Christian spirituality. However, Kidd's early interest in creative writing resurfaced in her forties, and she took creative writing classes, eventually writing a short story that became the basis for her best-selling first novel,* The Secret Life of Bees. *Both* The Secret Life of Bees *and her second novel,* The Mermaid Chair, *explore the spiritual growth of their female protagonist.*

[Sue Monk] Kidd is one of America's most popular contemporary writers. Since the publication of her breakthrough novel *The Secret Life of Bees* (2002), Kidd has become recognized for her examination of such themes as the healing power of love, the feminine quest for self-identity, the iniquities of racial bigotry, relationships between women, and the search for spiritual meaning in a secular age. A devout Christian, Kidd has also published a series of memoirs detailing the development of her religious faith and her search for a feminist strain of Christianity that breaks with fundamentalist tradition.

Contemporary Literary Criticism, "Sue Monk Kidd," vol. 267, ed. Jeffrey W. Hunter. Detroit: Gale, 2008, pp. 183–84. Copyright © 2012 by The Gale Group. All rights reserved. Reproduced by permission.

Biographical Information

Kidd was born in Sylvester, Georgia. Inspired by her father's storytelling, she spent much of her childhood writing, but stopped at the age of sixteen to focus on a future career in nursing. After earning her degree from Texas Christian University, Kidd worked as a nurse at St. Joseph's Hospital in Fort Worth, Texas, and was later an instructor at the Medical College of Georgia. In the early 1970s she became interested in spirituality, psychology, and mythology (particularly the works of psychologist Carl Jung and Catholic writer Thomas Merton) and began writing again, focusing on personal nonfiction. She published freelance articles and essays about her experiences and spiritual journey, eventually becoming a contributing editor to *Guideposts* magazine. Kidd has described her first book, *God's Joyful Surprise* (1987), as "a spiritual memoir which chronicled my early experiences with contemplative Christian spirituality." When she was in her forties, she moved away from fundamentalist Christianity and her nonfiction writing became more oriented towards feminist religious studies. Meanwhile, she retained a deep desire to pen stories. She took courses in fiction writing at Emory University and Sewanee University, and attended the Bread Loaf Writers' Conference. The fruit of these efforts was a short story titled "The Secret Life of Bees," which was published in the University of Tulsa's *Nimrod International Journal of Prose and Poetry*. "The Secret Life of Bees" garnered the Katherine Anne Porter Prize for Fiction (second place) at the annual *Nimrod* Literary Awards and was included in the 1994 edition of *Best American Short Stories*. The short story's success prompted Kidd to expand the work into her first novel. *The Secret Life of Bees* became a bestseller and won the SEBA [Southeast Booksellers Association] Book of the Year Award and the Southeastern Library Association Fiction Award; it was nominated for an International IMPAC Dublin Literary Award as well as the Orange Broadband Prize for Fiction. Kidd's follow-up novel, *The Mer-*

maid Chair (2005), received the Quill Award for General Fiction and also achieved bestsellerdom. In 2006 the governor of South Carolina awarded Kidd the Order of the Palmetto, the state's highest civilian honor. Kidd lives near Charleston, South Carolina, with her husband, Sanford Kidd, and serves as writer-in-residence at the Sophia Institute, an organization devoted to spiritual and creative growth.

Her Major Works

Kidd's fiction focuses on women who embark upon journeys of self-discovery after dissociating themselves from problematic relationships with men. During the course of her narratives, her female characters learn about themselves and uncover secrets from the pasts of their loved ones while developing a newfound sense of psychological and spiritual fortitude. Set in South Carolina in 1964 and inspired by the author's memories of the civil rights movement, *The Secret Life of Bees* is the story of fourteen-year-old Lily Owens, who has been raised by her abusive father, T. Ray, and their black servant, Rosaleen Daise. Lily's father blames her for the death of her mother, who was killed when Lily was only four years old. Eventually, Lily and Rosaleen run away from T. Ray and the police, who have beaten Rosaleen for trying to vote. Not knowing where to go, they heed the words written on the back of the cross Lily's mother once wore and head for Tiburon, South Carolina. In Tiburon they find Black Madonna Honey, an apiary run by three black sisters—August, June, and May Boatwright—who allow Lily and Rosaleen to stay with them. At the apiary Lily finally finds contentment; as she learns about the bees from the sisters, she develops a more mature perspective on her own life, and eventually discovers the truth behind her mother's death. *The Secret Life of Bees* was adapted for the stage by Tracy Stephenson Shaffer at Louisiana State University in 2004, and was adapted for the screen by writer-director Gina Prince-Bythewood in 2008.

Sue Monk Kidd attends the October 6, 2008, premiere of the film adaptation of her novel The Secret Life of Bees. © Mark Savage/Corbis.

The Mermaid Chair concerns Jessie Sullivan, a middle-aged housewife and part-time artist who is drawn back to her childhood home after receiving some disturbing news about her estranged mother. Leaving behind Hugh—her loyal, though slightly controlling husband—Jessie ventures back to tiny Egret Island, located off the coast of South Carolina. Upon her return, Jessie finds that her extraordinarily devout mother, Nelle, has cut off her finger for reasons unknown. Jessie suspects that her mother's descent into madness may have to do with her father's tragic death over thirty years ago, for which Jessie has always blamed herself. Her quest for answers leads her to the local monastery, where even more mysteries await her. There she finds a strange chair fashioned with the image of a saint who was once a mermaid, as well as a young monk, Brother Thomas, who is on the verge of taking his final vows. In meeting him, Jessie finds a passion she thought was lost and begins to feel a reawakening of her emotions, sensuality, and artistic vision. Kidd explores similar personal quests in her spiritually informed nonfiction, which includes *God's Joyful Surprise* and *When the Heart Waits* (1990). Another nonfiction work, *The Dance of the Dissident Daughter* (1996), examines Kidd's move away from the patriarchal dominion of her Southern Baptist background toward a nontraditional, feminist form of Christianity. *Firstlight* (2006), a collection of her early essays, provides valuable insight into the preliminary stages of her spirituality.

Critical Reception for Kidd's Work

Kidd's work has received a largely favorable response from reviewers. For example, they have lauded her nonfiction for providing accessible and moving insights into the issue of spirituality in the modern world, and have praised her novels for their authentic details. Specifically, they have highlighted the skill with which she creates a sense of time and place in her fiction, and have applauded her complex representation of the

Gullah people—the descendents of African American slaves who live on the southeastern coast of the United States. The religious subtext of her fiction has been a source of scholarly interest, especially with regard to the motif of the Black Madonna in *The Secret Life of Bees* and its theological counterparts throughout history. Some commentators have compared the references to the Virgin Mary in the Gospels with the figure of the Black Madonna in Kidd's novel, while others have interpreted Kidd's Madonna as part of her overall preoccupation with the spiritual aspect of female identity and the archetypal concept of the eternal feminine. "[T]he Black Madonna also serves as psychological archetype of an indomitable spirit, a soul not defeated by the persecutions of slavery," claimed critic Catherine B. Emanuel, ". . . Lily and Rosaleen escape their patriarchal home to find sanctuary in this matriarchal one." In addition, critics have identified a reference to one of Kidd's major theological influences, the monk and author Thomas Merton, in the character of Brother Thomas in *The Mermaid Chair*. Although most reviewers have commended Kidd's depiction of African American characters, some have faulted her work for propagating an idealized and sentimentalized stereotype common among white authors. Applying author Toni Morrison's linguistic interpretation of the issue of race to *The Secret Life of Bees*, commentator Linda Iraggi Larsen stated: "Missing from Kidd's romanticized novel are contributing factors that affect race, such as economics, class, women's issues, and differences between urban and rural settings, which leave her characters dislocated from a tangible, sociological framework." Despite such criticisms, Kidd maintains a devoted readership worldwide.

Kidd Took Creative Risks in Writing *The Secret Life of Bees*

Monica Dutcher

Monica Dutcher is the executive editor and cofounder of Stu-dioSashay, an editorial and design concern, and former executive editor of Sashay *magazine.*

Sue Monk Kidd developed a passion for writing at an early age but shelved the idea for a number of years as she pursued a more practical career, Dutcher reports in the following article. When she returned to creative writing later in life, Kidd took a methodical approach, attending creative writing classes and writers conferences, Dutcher explains. It took Kidd almost four years to write The Secret Life of Bees, *her best-selling and award-winning first novel. Kidd is not only a diligent writer, she is also a courageous one, one who takes creative risks, Dutcher claims, and praises Kidd for taking on the risky topics of racism and feminine struggle.*

"**I** love the water," says the Georgia native. "An ideal day involves taking a walk beside the water and reading—and writing without a deadline, without any pressure for it to succeed or not succeed. I don't need anything flashy or exotic. Just the rhythms of life."

Kidd says she began with an innate desire to be a writer, an inborn affinity that grew later in life to the point of artistic conviction. "It [writing] became my necessary fire. Perhaps we're all looking for that—for that thing that engages you and brings you alive," she explores. "Your necessary fire is not only necessary for you; it is necessary for the world itself . . . One of the more powerful outbreaks of happiness and meaning in your life will occur when you pair your passion and the world's need."

While in college, however, Kidd turned her back on her passion, succumbing to the conservative idea of pursuing something else to fall back on. But the writer in her wouldn't be squelched. At 29, Kidd describes, she began to feel "an internal sense of exile, a kind of homesickness for [her] own place of belonging in the world."

And so, in 1988, Kidd published her first book, *God's Joyful Surprise*, which describes the beginnings of her searches in spirituality, an element of life that Kidd says is intimately woven with creativity. "It [spirituality] is definitely a large part of my life," she affirms. "Creativity and spirituality come from the same place—deep in the soul. Creativity is a conversation that we have with our own soul."

In her second book, *When the Heart Waits* (1990), Kidd delves further into the nature of mid-life spiritual transformation, and in her third, a memoir entitled *The Dance of the Dissident Daughter* (1996), she navigates the connection between spirituality and feminist theology.

While Kidd's work sparked intensive conversation in religious and feminine circles, the poised, steel magnolia of a writer secretly (as Kidd often jokes, there's always a secret in the South, especially within families) kept a finger on the pulse of fiction. In 1992, she wrote the first chapter of *The Secret Life of Bees* (2002) and took it to a writer's conference, a daunting affair for Kidd given that she had never published a word of fiction.

After reading Kidd's chapter, a teacher at the conference told Kidd that it didn't have "novel potential" and would be best developed as a short story. Although this is not exactly what Kidd had hoped to hear, she wasn't defeated—in fact, she was ignited, shelving *The Secret Life of Bees* (for four more years) and promptly dedicating herself to what she viewed as an apprenticeship in fiction writing.

Author Sue Monk Kidd accepts the American Place Theatre's Literature to Life Award on April 27, 2004, at the New York Society for Ethical Culture. © Lawrence Lucier/FilmMagic.

Becoming a Novelist

Kidd enrolled in a graduate writing course at Emory University, and studied at Sewanee, Bread Loaf and other writers' conferences. She wrote and published short stories in small literary journals; she practiced her creative writing muscle just as an athlete would train for her sport. "I became a novelist by jumping in over my head and erring on the side of audacity," states Kidd, who, in reaching for nothing short of excellence, grounded yet propelled herself by asking, "What does my work serve?" instead of "How can I serve my work?"

In 1996, Kidd was invited to read fiction at the New York City Art Club. The event organizers asked her to read "something Southern," which sent Kidd searching . . . and searching for something that fit the bill. She came across that first chapter of *The Secret Life of Bees* and she questioned herself: "Should I revisit this?" Believing in her heart that the piece was poised to be something more, Kidd selected it for the reading—and what a smart selection it was. After the reading, a literary agent approached her, saying, "I sure hope that's the first chapter of your novel."

For the next three and a half years, Kidd immersed herself in the life and journey of 14-year-old Lily Owens, the protagonist in *The Secret Life of Bees* who runs away with her housekeeper in 1964 South Carolina to find refuge in the home of three black beekeeping sisters: August, May, and June Boatwright. The juxtaposition of a commune of strong, spiritual black women and a historically dark Southern landscape makes a bold statement about the very mettle of women, their cultural roots and their steadfastness in the divine. In the novel, this is especially illustrated by Kidd's intriguing use of the black Madonna, a statue of which is prominently displayed in the Boatwrights' home.

In a 2010 commencement address at Scripps College, Kidd quoted a *Secret Life of Bees* passage about the black Madonna: "One day August Boatwright says to Lily, '[The black Madonna] is something inside of you. When you're unsure of yourself, when you start pulling back into small living and into doubt, she's the one inside of you saying get up from there and be the glorious girl you are,'" Kidd read. "That voice sits in your head all day long saying 'Lily don't be afraid. I am enough—we are enough.'"

Due to its depth of storytelling, eloquent manipulation of language and empowering themes and metaphors, *The Secret Life of Bees* has sold more than 6 million copies, spent more than two and a half years on the *New York Times* bestseller list, been published in 35 countries, produced on stage in New York by The American Place Theater and adapted by Fox Searchlight into a major motion picture, which won the People's Choice and the NAACP [National Association for the Advancement of Colored People] Image awards for Best Picture.

Kidd's knack for fiction writing didn't dull after *The Secret Life of Bees*. Her second novel, *The Mermaid Chair* (2005), sold nearly 2 million copies, reached number one on the *New York Times* bestseller list, won the 2005 Quill Award for General Fiction, and was produced as a television movie by Lifetime. Set on a South Carolina barrier island, *The Mermaid Chair* tells the story of 42-year-old Jessie Sullivan, a married woman who falls in love with a Benedictine monk, a plot inspired by an image described by one of Kidd's friends who had returned from a trip to England. That image was a chair, located in a church, ornately carved with mermaids. The incongruity of the most sensual mythical creature on sacred ground piqued Kidd, who immediately knew she had her second book.

The Courage to Write About Racism

While Kidd's success is largely a product of her discipline to perfecting creative composition, her achievements are also a testament to her courage to shine light on unflattering moments in Southern history and on complex feminine emotion and struggle. "It's a very intimate experience, to write. It can be terrifying to put your work out there," she admits. But it's a "risk" worth taking because fiction, she says, is what connects us, makes us truly feel like we belong to the family of earth as opposed to a conglomerate of self-serving individuals. "Understanding one's particular genius, one's particular purpose in the community, is going to be perhaps the most indispensable ethic in the years ahead," says Kidd.

Perhaps this brings us back to that serene shore along the Carolina coast, to that plot of land that Kidd found so inspiring. Here, everything is connected—nothing is left without a purpose. Here, there are rhythms and patterns in tides and on beach towels, in nature and among people.

What's your necessary fire? The world is waiting.

The Secret Life of Bees and Coming of Age

Lily Is More Interested in Her Own Problems than in the Racial Turmoil Around Her

Ann-Janine Morey

Ann-Janine Morey is associate vice provost of the Department of Cross-Disciplinary Studies at James Madison University.

In The Secret Life of Bees *Sue Monk Kidd depicts the tensions in the South following the passage of the Civil Rights Act but does so in an unconvincing way, Morey contends in the following review. The complex issue of racism takes secondary importance to Lily's coming of age and search for a mother figure, Morey maintains.*

Ten years ago [in the early 90's] Sue Monk Kidd was a traditionally grounded Christian writer. But like her engaging narrator Lily Owens, Kidd is on a spiritual journey, heralded by her 1996 nonfiction work *The Dance of the Dissident Daughter* and confirmed in this captivating first novel [*The Secret Life of Bees*] about love and forgiveness. Guided by bees and a group of women devoted to a black Madonna, 14-year-old Lily Owens embarks upon a spiritual quest that carries her through the shadow of racism and her own spiritual suffering and brings her to adulthood.

Civil Rights Forms the Background

The context for her quest is South Carolina in 1964, a transformative year for civil rights. America had survived the fury and sorrow of 1963: the murder of Medgar Evers, the Bir-

Ann-Janine Morey, "The Secret Life of Bees," *Christian Century*, vol. 120, no. 4, February 22, 2003, pp. 68–70. Copyright © 2003 by the Christian Century. "The Secret Life of Bees, by Sue Monk Kidd" by Ann-Janine Morey is reprinted by permission from the February 22, 2003 issue of the *Christian Century*.

mingham church bombing and the assassination of John F. Kennedy. The next year brought the passage of the Civil Rights Act and the murder of three civil rights workers. Against this backdrop and often in conversation with these events, Lily and Rosaleen, a black woman who acts as her stand-in mother, flee the dubious charms of Sylvan, South Carolina.

Lily is running away from her father, T-Ray, who seems to care more for his dog than his daughter. She is an articulate, socially awkward teenager whose memory of her mother comes from her fourth year, when her mother was killed in a domestic dispute. Lily suspects she may be partially responsible for her mother's death, and her guilty hunger for parental love is the emotional axis of the novel.

When Rosaleen gets arrested during her attempt to register to vote, Lily liberates her from the hospital where she has been incarcerated, and the fugitives make their way to Tiburon, South Carolina. There a trio of bee-keeping sisters, May, June and August, whose self-sufficient business produces Black Madonna honey and a remarkable alternative religious community, takes them in. In the sitting room of the house is a wooden statue of a black Madonna, rescued from an old ship prow. A faded red heart is painted on her breast, and she extends her fisted arm "like she could straighten you out if necessary." Every evening the sisters kneel and pray before this figure, whom they call "Our Lady of Chains," creating their own liturgy and rituals from a blend of Catholicism, slave stories, African traditions, Judaism and any number of meditative traditions. Every year the household observes "Mary Day," and the legend of the chains is reenacted with music, dance and food.

Lily, a sometime Baptist, is captivated by the woman-centered practices of the "calendar sisters." She learns that traditionally the Madonna is sometimes associated with honey and beekeeping, and she discovers how the creative life of the hive becomes a symbol of the living heart of the great Mother.

An African American woman is beaten by a sheriff and arrested for standing in line to register to vote in Selma, Alabama, in January 1965. © AP Images/Horace Cort.

The hum of the hive is the "oldest sound there was. Souls flying away." Once August's mother heard the bees "singing the words to the Christmas story right out of the gospel of Luke." Indeed, the hidden throb of the hive swells from the place where "everything is sung to life." Like the life-force of bee-hum, Mary's spirit is "hidden everywhere. Her heart a cup of fierceness tucked among ordinary things," observes Lily.

Lily Is Self-Absorbed

Imperfectly integrated with her spiritual journey is Lily's account of racism, as Rosaleen prepares again to register to vote, and a neighbor is arrested on trumped-up assault charges during an altercation with local racists. Because Lily is so absorbed in her own emotional deprivation, these events finally take on secondary importance, and there is a tidiness to the novel's conclusion that does not do justice to the powerful forces that have been invoked. It's understandable why sister

June might have been suspicious of this white girl who wants to listen in to their lives and finally take up residence. It's still all about her at the end.

Despite the historical realism of the novel, there is a fairy-tale quality to it. Three wise black women rule a magical universe of sweetness and organic communion and offer their healing to weary travelers. Lily is an appealing narrator, but sometimes she seems much younger than 14 and sometimes much older. August is given to speeches telling us wise things we might better have seen than heard, and I found Mary's identity as the mother of sorrows unconvincing.

But these are minor criticisms. Though adults will find *The Secret Life of Bees* a satisfying read, the clarity of the novel's prose will make it appealing to a younger audience as well. I'll be passing it on to my middle-school daughter for its warm invitation to think about mother love and forgiveness.

The Secret Life of Bees
Traces the Spiritual Growth
of a Teenage Girl

Susan Andersen

Susan Andersen is an English teacher, writer, and consultant for higher education.

Lily passes through several stages of spiritual growth in The Secret Life of Bees, *asserts Andersen in the following essay. Lily's first step toward transformation occurs when she runs away from her father to escape abuse, Andersen explains. Lily finds safety and comfort with the Boatwright sisters, and this gives her a period of time when she can contemplate her previous life and beliefs. As the truth about her past is revealed, Lily learns that her mother loved her, which gives her the strength to forgive both herself and her mother, the critic suggests. Finally, Lily is able to view her father with compassion, forgiving him as well.*

Lily Owens, the fourteen-year-old heroine of *The Secret Life of Bees*, has a tragic personal story that includes accidentally shooting her mother and living with an abusive father. She runs away with her African-American nanny, Rosaleen, whose story is also heading towards tragedy. It is not until Lily stays with the Boatwrights that shelearns any alternative stories to the dead-end ones that she has grown up with. The book chronicles the way in which Lily, or any person, can change the tale of their lives.

Kidd Reinvents the Female Role

In the tradition of the Southern women writers she keeps company with—Carson McCullers, Alice Walker, Harper Lee—

Susan Andersen, "Critical Essay on *The Secret Life of Bees*," in *Novels for Students*, vol. 27, ed. Ira Mark Milne. Detroit: Gale, 2008, pp. 226–49. Copyright © 2008 by The Gale Group. All rights reserved. Reproduced by permission.

[Sue Monk] Kidd reenvisions the female role, expanding it even as far as embracing a female image of God. Indeed, in her collection of essays, *Firstlight*, Kidd has said, "Discovering our personal stories is a spiritual quest. Without such stories we cannot be fully human . . ." In order for Lily to find her own story, she has to hear the stories of other women, who have blazed the trail before her.

When Lily meets June's suitor, Neil, he asks where she comes from. Lily realizes this sort of introductory phrase comes from the desire all people have of fitting their stories together. To begin with, she has no way to connect her background to that of Neil or the Boatwright sisters because she is white and fourteen, and they are African-American and adult. August becomes a sort of mother and teacher who helps Lily resurrect herself by initiating her into a new culture, with new female stories about the secret life of bees and the Black Madonna. At Lily's first meeting of the Daughters of Mary, August retells the story of Our Lady of Chains, saying, "Stories have to be told or they die, and when they die, we can't remember who we are or why we're here."

When August asks Lily what her favorite things are, she mentions writing. She is seen with paper and pen constantly, writing about her experience and making up exotic stories. Her facility with images and reflection is remarkable for a young girl; her English teacher has told her she should be a writer, and that is what she dreams of. When Zach is in jail, the only consolation she can think of is to tell him she will write it down and tell his story. She creates stories for her friends to star in, and August, in a way, allows Lily to change her own story.

What story needs changing? In *The History of Southern Women's Literature*, Ann Goodwyn Jones speaks of the limited roles for Southern women that have always been the subject of Southern women writers—for Caucasians, "lady, belle, Christian yeowoman of the middle class, spinster, and trash;

for blacks, mammy, mulatta, Christian yeowoman of the middle class, loudmouth, and whore." The list is limited, but Harper Lee's heroine, Scout [in *To Kill a Mackingbird*], manages to break free, as does Celie in [Alice Walker's] *The Color Purple*, along with a host of Southern heroines, like Scarlett O'Hara [in Margaret Mitchell's *Gone with the Wind*]. Sue Monk Kidd herself wanted to be a writer from an early age, like her character, Lily. But, she notes in *Firstlight*, that in a small Georgia town in the 1950s, she only knew of four careers: "teacher, nurse, secretary, and housewife." So she chose nursing and stayed in that profession through her twenties, though it wasn't what she wanted. The rest of her life, she continues, was a series of moves to undo the "Collective They," or the expectations of society that keep one from living an authentic life. Kidd says more in *Firstlight* about writing and storytelling as important tools of "soul-making," for when people share their stories, they come to find "we are all one story." In *The Secret Life of Bees* the reader identifies with Lily's story, sometimes in the particulars, but more importantly, in the stages of her spiritual growth. In all her books, fiction or nonfiction, Kidd maps out the territory surrounding the transformation of the soul. In *The Dance of the Dissident Daughter*, for instance, Kidd tells of an autobiographical journey from strict Southern Baptist to a religion that embraces feminist theology. In *When the Heart Waits*, she talks about the universal stages of growth as the three-fold cycle of waiting: separation, transformation, and emergence. The stages of waiting serve to illuminate Lily's growth from false to true story.

In the beginning, Lily doesn't know what it is to be female: "I felt half the time I was impersonating a girl instead of really being one." She bites her fingernails, wears Pentecostal dresses—dresses that look severely modest or religious rather than stylish—and cannot get into charm school because she has no mother to present her a rose at graduation. Neither her father nor Rosaleen can help her with her adolescent problems, and even the Baptist church has no female role model for her, except Mary at Christmas. When Lily finds the picture of the Black Madonna among her mother's possessions, she is intrigued by its mystery. August tells her later that all people need an image of God that looks like them, so they can feel divine. The Daughters of Mary connect with their black, female God. Lily, though not African-American, finally has a female image that can make her begin to feel both divine and loved.

Spiritual Growth Aided by Contemplation

The first step of transformation, according to Kidd in *When the Heart Waits*, is separation, often through crisis. Lily is forced to run away to save Rosaleen and herself from being abused. She runs to the only place she knows of, Tiburon, the place on the Black Madonna postcard. In this stage of separation, one leaves behind their false life. This may take some time, as it does for Lily; even though she arrives in a different place in one day, it takes her all summer to drop many of her false ideas—her inherited prejudices about African-American people, for instance, and her own belief that she is bad or will be further abused if she tells the truth.

According to Kidd, in the same book, the transformation stage is helped by withdrawing into a safe cocoon where one may let go. Lily says the first week at August's was "pure relief," a "time-out." Her first prayer to Our Lady of Chains is that she put a curtain of protection around the farm so no one can find them. Lily delays talking to August about her mother until the end of the summer. This appears to be a mistake on Lily's part, but although August knows who she is all the time, she never rushes Lily's confession. She tells her: "There's a fullness of time for things, Lily. You have to know when to prod and when to be quiet, when to let things take their course."

Mill Creek Baptist Church, North Carolina, 1944. The Secret Life of Bees *reflects Sue Monk Kidd's journey from the patriarchal Southern Baptist Church to a feminist spirituality.* © Gabriel Benzur/Time & Life Pictures/Getty Images.

The time-out, spending time with the Daughters of Mary and working as a respected apprentice beekeeper with August, gives Lily a chance to think deeply about her life, to discard the lies she has been told and to see the truth that her new friends show her. Kidd continues in *When the Heart Waits* to describe incubation as a time when one can hold tensions creatively, to live one's questions. Lily is alive because she asks countless questions about the way things are: Why did God make different skin colors? Why do Baptists try to convert Catholics? Why don't white Christians accept African-American Christians? Why do Caucasians think African Americans are not intelligent or handsome when they are? Why are African-American women, who are so powerful, lowest on the social totem pole?

Kidd says of herself in *The Dance of the Dissident Daughter* that her own contemplative experiences put her at odds with her Baptist background, because contemplative religion favors the personal experience of God over dogma (accepted religious views). Kidd began to recognize that the ultimate religious authority was the divine voice in her own soul. The same realization happens to Lily, for from the beginning, her own spiritual insights mean more to her than what she learns from Brother Gerald's pulpit, for instance. She has mystical experiences with Our Lady of Chains and with the bees. In the Boatwright parlor, Lily first lays eyes on the Black Mary who is the Madonna of Slaves. Mary has the power to get out of the chains that bind—to take her followers to freedom. Lily is immediately attracted to her. Mary's smile speaks to her soul: "*Lily Owens, I know you down to the core.*"

The Dance of the Dissident Daughter asserts that a woman must trust her own feminine source and that it is a place inside that feels ancient. Lily calls the Black Mary in the parlor "older than old." Lily also experiences something ancient in beekeeping. August connects making honey to everything biblical and ancient, from fertility to death to resurrection. The fact that the queen bee runs the hive and that women make better beekeepers, according to Big Mama, connects it to the traditional power of women.

Lily Discovers Her True and Best Self

Kidd mentions *When the Heart Waits* how knowing God as a mother in her own spiritual journey, allowed "the wedding of my soul with creation." Similarly, August shows Lily how to appreciate nature, how not to be afraid of bees, to give them love, so they won't sting. Lily does, and feels that she becomes one with the bees, floating, immune to everything. When May is buried, she feels the bees hum through the whole earth and souls flying away to heaven. Lily is consoled by the natural world, as when she goes to the river while she is mourning.

The stage of emergence, described in *When the Heart Waits*, has to do with forming a new relationship with others based on a renewed relationship with God. Knowing God as mother, says Kidd, brings us to greater intimacy with God, because it is an image of a caring and nourishing God rather than a punishing God. In her distress, Lily imagines a door in the Madonna's belly. She envisions crawling into a hidden room in Mary's abdomen, as though she is Mary's child. The reenactment of the legend of Mary's captivity in chains coincides with Lily's dark night of the soul when she smashes honey jars on the wall and falls asleep at Mary's feet. But "What is bound will be unbound," as the Mary Day ritual says. The climax of the festivity is bathing the statue in honey and taking off the Lady's chains. When Lily receives the picture of Deborah with herself as a baby, Lily begins to lose her own chains, for she finally realizes that her mother loved her. She forgives both herself and her mother. Lily's emerging intimacy with God leads her to experience intimacy with others.

Lily further exhibits this final stage of growth in her confrontation with T. Ray when he comes to get her. She is different, stands up for herself, and asserts her authority. The emergent stage is characterized by a new compassion, says Kidd. Lily sees her father in a new light, as someone who once loved and became cruel through disappointment. She calls him Daddy, thus acknowledging her connection to him. Once she makes it past the obstacle of forgiving her parents, she is ready for the final truth that August has to teach her: God, or Our Lady, is not outside, but inside. Lily affirms this: "I feel her in unexpected moments, her Assumption into heaven happening in places inside me."

Kidd says in her essay, "The Crucible of Story" in *Firstlight* that storytelling is soul-making, but it requires a risk of stepping into the shadows to find the angels there. Lily has demonstrated soul-making to us by reclaiming the shadows of her story and finding the angels within it at the same time. She would like to get her father to say that she didn't shoot her mother, but she accepts that even if she did, she can forgive herself and move on to better stories, because her mothers, both the human and the divine, know her true and best self.

The Black Madonna in *The Secret Life of Bees* Symbolizes the Mother Within Us

Catherine B. Emanuel

Catherine B. Emanuel teaches creative writing and the history of literature at Reinhardt University in Alpharetta, Georgia.

According to Emanuel in the following essay, Lily's quest in The Secret Life of Bees *is not only for a mother figure, but also for a religion that is meaningful to her. The American South of the 1960s was a racist and patriarchal society, and conventional religion was also patriarchal, Emanuel explains. Living with the Boatwright sisters, Lily learns about the Black Madonna and embraces a matriarchal religion that helps her to find God within herself.*

In her 2002 novel, *The Secret Life of Bees*, former *Guidepost* magazine contributor Sue Monk Kidd departs from Baptist conservatism to produce a fourteen-year-old heroine, Lily, who finds solace and spirituality in a black woman's face. Set in 1960s South Carolina, this novel captures the period's racial prejudice and white patriarchy but reproduces the time's rebellious fervor as well. As Lily faces the revelation of a sheriff who doles out injustice to her housekeeper, Rosaleen, and a Southern Baptist religion that reinforces the tyranny of her father, T. Ray, she longs for a mother. This search takes psychological and archetypal turns as Lily confronts her own implication in her mother's death. Her only link to the mother she never really knew is a picture of a Black Madonna with a

Catherine B. Emanuel, "The Archetypal Mother: The Black Madonna in Sue Monk Kidd's *The Secret Life of Bees*," *West Virginia University Philological Papers*, vol. 52, 2005, pp. 115–22. Copyright © 2005 by West Virginia University. All rights reserved. Reproduced by permission.

South Carolina town printed beneath it. Kidd ties all the frayed strands of past to present for Lily in the home of three black beekeepers—May, June, and August—who have their own Black Madonna, whom they declare is "blessed among women." Throughout the novel, Kidd scrupulously ties all her symbols, most importantly those of the lily and bees, to this black icon. Thus, Lily's search for an archetypal mother expands from a quest for psychological identity to a quest for a religion that offers some reflection of herself.

A Search for a Feminine God

In 1996 Kidd wrote her spiritual autobiography, *The Dance of the Dissident Daughter*, in which she recounts her own attempt to find a feminine face of God. This search sent her to visit monasteries, to read religious texts extensively, and to denounce the patriarchy of the Southern Baptist Church. An unlikely feminist, she speaks at length about a woman's plight in both conventional society and orthodox religion. As she puts it:

> When she finally lets herself *feel* the limits and injustices of female life and admits how her own faith tradition has contributed to that, when she at last stumbles in the dark hole made by the absence of a Divine Feminine presence . . . this woman will become pregnant with herself, with the symbolic female-child who will, if given a chance, grow up to reinvent the woman's life.

Just as Toni Morrison did in *The Bluest Eye*, Kidd discusses the psychological damage of women's exclusion, exclusion from representation in society's power positions and in her viewpoint, exclusion from nearly all church images and stories. As she explains, "We find genuine female authority within when we become the 'author' of our own identity. By taking the journey to the feminine soul, we 'authorize' ourselves" [Kidd states in *The Dance of the Dissident Daughter*]. As she recounts in her own autobiography and again in the spiritual and psychological voyage of her heroine Lily, this writing a woman's self into being is often arduous. Though she does not offer Lily a safe or sweet early life, she does jolt her protagonist into a new way of thinking and a new way of interpreting old stories.

Lily and Rosaleen Seek New Identities

Throughout *The Secret Life of Bees*, Lily is forced to examine institutional ideas of justice, and these revised thoughts inspire new ways of being, both for Lily and for Rosaleen. First, Lily discovers that the institution of local justice, the sheriff's office, only metes out fairness to white people. When Rosaleen goes to register to vote, she finds her path impeded by white men who want to denounce Civil Rights' progress. Empowered by the Civil Rights Act of 1963, she dumps her snuff can spit onto their shoes. When she is arrested after being beaten by these men, the sheriff opens her cell to these same men so they can continue the abuse. Though Lily had suffered through her own persecution at the hands of T. Ray, whose favorite form of punishment consisted in making his daughter kneel bare-kneed for hours on Martha White grits, Lily realizes that Rosaleen's injustice can produce life-threatening consequences. Fleeing from her hometown police after breaking Rosaleen out of her hospital jail, Lily concocts new stories for the many people who question a black woman and a teenaged white girl's being together on the road.

In these new identities, Rosaleen and Lily try on different personalities as they become part of life in the beekeepers' pink house. This search for a new identity assumes archetypal dimensions. As Jungian psychologist Marion Woodman points out, "If we leave our father's house, we have to make ourselves self-reliant. Otherwise, we just fall into another father's house." Rosaleen and Lily find their road to self-awareness paved by the calendar sisters, May, June and August. These names span a time frame of both sowing and reaping, spring to late summer. Appropriately enough, the harvest name, August be-

This 2004 photograph shows a statue of the Black Madonna in Le Puy Cathedral, a national monument of France, in Le Puy-en-Velay, Auvergne. © P. Deliss/Godong/Corbis.

friends Lily, but not in the ways of the father. She does not deliver edicts and punishment like an Old Testament God or a T. Ray; instead, she lets Lily find her own way in her own time to the facts of her mother's death. As Nancy Chodorow points out in *The Reproduction of Mothering: Psychoanalysis and the Sociology of Gender,* "The basic feminine sense of self is connected to the world; the basic masculine sense is separate." If we could borrow from the psychological to parallel the spiritual, Kidd describes the difference this way:

> Patriarchy had majored in divine transcendence, which means separateness from the material universes—being above all, beyond or apart from it. Divine Immanence, on the other hand, is divinity here, near and now, inherent in the material stuff of life.

Divine Immanence for her represents the matriarchal view of spirituality, the interconnectedness of life, nature, and spirit.

August and Lily become individual threads of an intricately woven spiritual and natural tapestry. Kidd captures this feeling of nature's pattern in an early scene where Lily steals into the night to unearth artifacts from her mother, included among which is "the funny wooden picture of Mary with the dark face." She caresses the few belongings her mother left her and then collapses into nature. In her words,

> When I looked up through the web of trees, the night fell over me, and for a moment I lost my boundaries, feeling like the sky was my own skin and the moon was my heart beating up there in the dark ... I undid the bottoms on my shirt and opened it wide, just wanting the night to settle on my skin, and that's how I fell asleep, lying there with my mother's things, with the air making moisture on my check, and the sky puckering with light.

The Bees Represent a Matriarchal Society

In the original incarnation of this novel, Kidd's 1993 short story aptly titled "The Secret Life of Bees," published in *The*

Nimrod International Journal, she provides a different motivation for Lily's night excursion. Instead of this voyage into the community of nature, Lily, this one aged thirteen instead of fourteen, sneaks from her father's house for a romantic tryst with her boyfriend, Sonny. In 1993 Kidd had embarked upon her own self-revelatory religious journey, but she had not yet abandoned the Southern Baptist Church or her role as writer for *Guidepost Magazine*. In other words, she was still allied with the instruments of patriarchy herself. In changing the story to Lily's search for mother in the novel, she moves her character from other-directedness to self-directedness, a hard turn left on the road to solace and spirituality, a move that parallels Kidd's own religious shift.

Throughout the novel resonate the sound and activities of a natural matriarchal society, that of bees. Each section's heading features the inner workings of this communal society. We are then constantly reminded of the symbol, not only through the work of the characters, but also through our introduction to all plot action. As [symbolism scholar] Hans Biedermann points out, "In the secular world the bee was a royal symbol, especially since the queen bee was long regarded as the king. It has been speculated that the French *fleur-de-lis* [lily] goes back to a stylized image of the bee." He further points to the belief in antiquity "that bees do not procreate their young but instead gather them up from the flowers they visit, making the bee a symbol for the Virgin Mary." In other words. Kidd corresponds all the major symbols of the novel, the bees, the lily, and the Black Madonna, to the Virgin Mary, at least that's one version of this icon in existence for hundreds, if not thousands, of years.

The Black Madonna has been around in some form, as dark pregnant woman, since 18,000 B.C. In such a case, she creates evidence of a pre-Christian matriarchal religion. In other words, she becomes a symbol, in some theories, of a community of women or like-believers worshipping figures of

45

a dark woman and embracing the concept of finding the god-like within themselves, for they see their inner selves mirrored in a woman's face. When August directs Lily to a queenless hive of bees, she explains, "You have to find a mother inside yourself. We all do." More than just emotional self-nourishing, this inner parenting assumes a spiritual comfort as well, for August tells Lily, "Our Lady is not some magical being out there somewhere, like a fairy godmother. She's not the statue in the parlor. She's something *inside* of you." She then tells her not to look without for God, but rather to look within. . . .

Conventional Religion Was Racist

In *The Secret Life of Bees*, T. Ray, whom Kidd equates with the patriarchal church, prohibits Lily's reading. Lily says, "he would half kill me," if someone even reported her reading to her father. She ponders further, "What kind of person is against *reading*?" Reading is self-empowerment, and reading produces questions and new interpretations. Just as the early Catholic Church had forbidden a parishioner's reading of scripture because this enlightened person might seek counsel directly with God, neither does T. Ray want Lily to question his authority. He sees society not as concentric circles but rather as a vertical line, a power structure competitive, not cooperative, in nature. For him and for the institutions supporting this hierarchical power structure, women and blacks have no place in the line-up.

In the 1960s South this patriarchal structure, reinforced by conventional religion, was also racist in nature. At the time Rosaleen is beaten by white men who find her uppity, she holds church fans she had taken from the church where she and Lily had rested, a church that would not have allowed her as a black woman to worship. To examine Christianity's role in the abuse of blacks would take another paper, but I do want to quote Frederick Douglass on this topic. A freed slave and abolitionist, Douglass knew first-hand the atrocities committed by slave owners, but he is clear to point out that the worst abuse occurred at the hands of the religious, for these men rationalized their harshness with text from the Bible. As he puts it,

> The religion of the South is a mere covering for the most horrid crimes—a justifier of the most appalling barbarity—a sanctifier of the most hateful frauds—and a dark shelter under which the darkest, foulest, grossest and most infernal deeds of slaveholders find the strongest protection.

Blacks then in America have had a complex relationship with the church whose ideology and texts on the one hand served to oppress them and on the other provided some comfort and solace, but only in a rewriting from white ideology.

An example of this rewriting is Rosaleen's personal religion typified by her altar, a "special shelf with a stub of candle, creek rocks, a reddish feather, and a piece of John the Conqueror root, and right in the center a picture of a woman, propped up without a frame." Lily describes this shelf as a "religion she'd [Rosaleen] made up for herself, a mixture of nature and ancestor worship." Note, however, that the center of the altar, a place generally reserved for pictures of Jesus, is a picture instead of Rosaleen's mother. In other words, her religion is woman-centered. In *Dance of the Dissident Daughter*, Kidd cites Dr. Beatrice Bruteau who likens the absolute reality, the I Am, with God and sees natural patterns within the many divine relationships exemplified in dance:

> When we see the dance, the dancer takes on expression, shape, immediacy, presence, and meaning for us. We can observe the relationship of the dance to the dancer, and we understand that the choreography is infinite. We cannot look at just one movement or one dance and say, that is the dance.

Or, if we borrow from William Butler Yeats, himself a mystic of sorts, we pose the question: "Who can tell the dancer

In this 1960 photograph, New Orleans curio vendor Sharif Khan displays items used in voodoo. He holds a box containing John the Conqueror root, one of the curios on the character Rosaleen's altar in The Secret Life of Bees. © AP Images/Nick Ut.

from the dance?" If all living things possess their own divinity, then we need not look up to find God, we need only to recognize that presence and revel in the dance of nature.

One facet of this acceptance of inward divinity instead involves coping with imperfection. After all, it's easy to perfect a deity that is light years away but quite a different matter to find God and perfection in the mirror. When Lily finally asks August about her mother, August gingerly tells her Deborah's story. This story, this making Deborah a real person, is Lily's first step in recognizing her part in her mother's death. She has then to see her mother as a person in order to feel her loss. Lily finds out that her mother left her father and her because she suffered from depression. August provides a coda to her revelation when she says, "Every person on the face of the earth makes mistakes, Lily. Every last one. We're all so human . . . There is nothing perfect . . . There is only life." Angered by her mother's abandonment, Lily smashes jars of honey and cuts herself in the process. She is now ready to find out the last part of Deborah's story, a story in which she as a small child played a principal role.

Throughout this whole novel of religious quest and struggle toward self-actualization and awareness, Kidd provides mirrors. Seeing what Sherry Ruth Anderson and Patricia Hopkins call Shekhinah, or "the feminine face of God" in the Black Madonna, Lily finds her spiritual center, the same feeling she had gotten from her bare-breasted night vigil. Through August, Lily sees a face her mother saw and faces a truth about her mother, the final portion of which T. Ray must deliver. When August presents Lily with more artifacts from her mother, she prefaces the unveiling by saying, "If *you* look in here, you're gonna see your mother's face looking back at you." Unfortunately for Lily, T Ray also sees Deborah's face when he looks at Lily. He wants to force her return. As the emblem for conventional religion and society's patriarchal struggle, he bullies, proving that he too is damaged by this power principle. For a few minutes, T. Ray sees before him the young wife who left him, here in the haven she had chosen, instead of his teenaged daughter. After slapping her across the face, he stands over Lily and screams, "Deborah . . . You're not leaving me again." Lying next to the Black Madonna that also had been knocked to the floor, Lily smells honey, the preservation rubbed into the icon's face and figure, and the same honey she herself had hurled into the wall venting her own anger at her mother's leaving her. In that moment Lily understands T. Ray. As she picks up Mary and rights her, T. Ray struggles to deal with his own actions. He illustrates the problem Kidd points out in *The Dance of the Dissident Daughter* when she writes, "Cut off from nature, we get sick inside." Patriarchy then inflicts psychological damage to the men who seem outwardly to profit from it.

If T. Ray typifies patriarchal punishment to maintain its vertical hierarchy, then August represents the subversion of that order and a return to nature, human nature most notably. Though she could have shamed him as she stands witness to his wrath against Lily, August considers his feelings. As Lily remembers from earlier conversations with August, "If you need something from somebody, always give that person a way to hand it to you." August wants Lily, she wants to nourish instead of starve her soul. T. Ray's one act of generosity, which he offers with a "Good riddance," is his letting Lily remain within this matriarchy, this earlier home of her mother. Before he leaves, however, Lily discovers that she herself had shot her mother. Though an accident, her death resulted from Lily's pulling the trigger. As Kidd has noted [in *Dance of the Dissident Daughter*], "The truth may set you free, but first if will shatter the safe, sweet way you live." On a firmer footing now, Lily absorbs the truth. She has grown into a person who can face the past and look to the future.

Lily then is allowed to flower in the seasonal house of May, June, and August. Nourished in the fertile soil of a Black

Madonna and an accepting, cooperative life and household, Lily becomes an integral part of the commune, the hive. She learns to mother herself and to discover the harmony of this life. Of her like-titled short story, Kidd has written, "One of the first short stories I published told the story of a southern girl named Lily who struggles to find the strength of her feminine wings in a world that routinely clips them." In this novel, however, Kidd allows her heroine flight, transcendence, and belonging.

Community Offers Lily a Place for Transformation

Amy Lignitz Harken

Amy Lignitz Harken is the associate minister at Community Christian Church in Kansas City, Missouri.

The Secret Life of Bees *is a classic coming of age novel, according to Harken in the following viewpoint. Like many coming of age novels, Sue Monk Kidd's first novel begins with its teenage protagonist leaving home in search of liberation and renewal, Harken states. However,* The Secret Life of Bees *is also about spirituality and community. The Boatwright sisters and the Daughters of Mary are symbols of a nurturing Christian community.*

You might read [*The Secret Life of Bees*] as a "coming of age" novel. Lily, a white, motherless fourteen-year-old girl, escapes a dull and difficult life with a hard and difficult father by running away to Tiburon, South Carolina. As Lily sets out on her quest of liberation and renewal, she takes with her Rosaleen, an African American woman who has been a stand-in caretaker since Lily was four, when Lily's birth mother died in an accidental shooting. Given Lily's age and spiritual awakening, *The Secret Life of Bees* is indeed about growing up and coming into one's own. You might notice her budding sexuality, her increasing awareness of the Divine, and her happy (eventually) inclusion in a group of women who draw strength from one another.

Amy Lignitz Harken, "Introduction," "Chapter 2: Earthly Mother," "Chapter 4: Daughter," "Chapter 5: Queen," "Chapter 6: Wife," in *Unveiling "The Secret Life of Bees."* St. Louis, MO: Chalice Press, 2005, pp. 1–2, 30–31, 61–64, 73–74, 77–81, 95–96, 98–99. Copyright © 2005 by Chalice Press. All rights reserved. Reproduced by permission.

As Lily and Rosaleen find themselves in the embrace of the "calendar sisters"—August, May, and June—other themes emerge, including the theme of presence. The novel is about divine presence and how we experience it, and about the presence of others and how salvation can be found there as well.

Celebrating Community

[Sue Monk] Kidd's book is about the divine, about religion, and about invocation. It might challenge the way you think about God. Instead of a male Father God, which many Christians find familiar, even comforting, Kidd's book revolves around the spirit of Mary, the mother of Jesus. Yet this book is not primarily concerned with Mary's role as Jesus' mother. Instead the focus is on Mary as a protector and guardian, Mary as the face of God, Mary as the mother of us all, Mary as the long-sufferer who understands all woe.

Although *The Secret Life of Bees* emphasizes Mary's presence in times of woe and in our own hearts, the sense of presence cannot be located in her alone. Characters are very much involved in the practice of being with one another, and absences are well noted. This book is as much about the human community as it is about communion with the Divine. Rosaleen is present for Lily while her mother is absent and her father emotionally absent. The calendar sisters are present for one another, and May's eventual physical absence is deeply felt. Lily and August are present for Zach in his crisis. Even Neil, who vows never to return to the Boatwright household after a fight with June, is present for the crisis of Zach's arrest. . . .

Missing Mothers

Much of *The Secret Life of Bees* revolves around the absence of Lily's mother. Lily is haunted by the only memory she has of Deborah—the day Deborah died. Even though Lily's memories of her mother are few and sketchy, Lily longs for a mother

The queen bee is the larger bee surrounded by drones, who are dependent upon her, their mother. © Redmond Durrell/Alamy.

and has definite ideas about what a mother should be, namely, *present*. The haunting memory and the secret longing for a mother keep Lily awake. The angry words of her father about her mother are Lily's motivation for leaving home, and a small physical remnant of her mother drives her to Tiburon, South Carolina. Even after she finds welcome in the home of the calendar sisters, the longing does not subside:

> The worst thing was lying there wanting my mother. That's how it had always been; my longing for her nearly always came late at night when my guard was down. I tossed on the sheets, wishing I could crawl into bed with her and smell her skin. I wondered: Had she worn thin nylon gowns to bed? Did she bobby-pin her hair? I could just see her, propped in bed. My mouth twisted as I pictured myself climbing in beside her and putting my head against her breast. I would put it right over her beating heart and listen. Mama, I would say. And she would look down at me and say, Baby, I'm right here.

By the end of the novel, as Lily reconciles in her heart with her biological mother, she realizes that she has many "mothers." Just as bees in a hive have their specific functions, the women in *The Secret Life of Bees* fill a variety of roles in the household and in Lily's life. Two main mother figures are August and Rosaleen, who are a study in contrasts. Lily compares each of them to the statue of the virgin Mary in the parlor:

> It was plain that Rosaleen had fire in her, too. Not hearth fire, like August, but fire that burns the house down, if necessary, to clean up the mess inside it. Rosaleen reminded me of the statue of Our Lady in the parlor, and I thought, If August is the red heart on Mary's chest, Rosaleen is the fist. . . .

Each woman in *The Secret Life of Bees* is a daughter. Rosaleen, whom we know primarily as one of Lily's two surrogate mothers, remembers and honors her own mother. She keeps and often beholds a photograph of her mother. She talks admiringly about how her mother labored long and hard to support her seven children. Rosaleen might not keep in touch with her siblings, but she remembers her hardworking mother.

Lily's other surrogate mother, August, also fondly remembers her mother and the household of love she created for her four daughters. Lily recognizes the longing in August's heart for her mother: "August set down the jar she was working on, and there was a mix of sorrow and amusement and longing across her face, and I thought, *She is missing her mother.*" Lily has no such luxury of fond remembrances and must navigate the role of daughter with only a few items her mother left: a pair of gloves, a photograph, a mysterious icon of Mary, and a remembered smell of cold cream.

Lily and Freedom

As a girl becomes a woman, she naturally tries to establish herself as independent of her mother. Girls try new fashions, new words, new dances. She may test the boundaries of what is acceptable. She may want to start spending time alone with boys. She may want to explore new career options. She may develop her own opinions about politics and world events. She may challenge her parents' basic understandings of right and wrong. As a girl comes into her own, she can perceive even the best mother as a constraint to her freedom. A girl can feel trapped by everything from her mother's taste in clothing to her moral code.

Without her biological mother, Lily undergoes a different struggle for freedom. Having escaped the "jar" of her home in Sylvan and the immediate threat of her father's wrath. Lily continues to be held captive by the longing for her mother—curiosity about her life and guilt associated with her death. . . . Lily's deep longing for a mother . . . plagues her and catches her off guard. When Lily and August check the beehives one day, the bees begin to alight on Lily, covering her body. Lily undergoes a mystical, euphoric experience in a field of clover:

> Then, without warning, all the immunity wore off, and I felt the hollow, spooned-out space between my navel and breast-bone begin to ache. The motherless place. I could see my mother in the closet, the stuck window, the suitcase on the floor. I heard the shouting, then the explosion. I almost doubled over. I lowered my arms, but I didn't open my eyes. How could I live the whole rest of my life knowing these things?

Lily does not long for just a mother: she longs for a home and a normal family life. Rosaleen warns Lily about getting too attached to the calendar sisters, particularly when their stay at the Boatwright household is premised on a lie. But Lily pleads with Rosaleen not to share their secret. Rosaleen accuses Lily of living in a "dream world," but Lily wants to keep her secret in order to stay and lead a "regular life."

Lily becomes trapped in a quandary. While she wants to preserve her "dream world," she also wants desperately to come clean with August, whom she has grown to love. Especially after Lily discovers that her mother had stayed at the Boatwright house, Lily yearns to talk with August about her mother and reveal the real reason she and Rosaleen came to Tiburon. But time and time again, her fears prevent the conversation.

Lily also longs for Zach. She harbors normal pubescent sexual desires for him, in addition to feelings of friendship. But the longing is compounded by the seeming impossibility of a relationship between a white girl and a black boy in 1964 South Carolina. Tied in with her feelings of longing is the strong determination not to settle down with anyone. Lily clings to possibility and to the freedom associated with it.

Captivity and liberation is a major theme in *The Secret Life of Bees*. The black Mary, "Our Lady of Chains," was a symbol of liberation to captive slaves. The highlight of Mary Day is a reenactment of her captivity and release. Rosaleen repeatedly struggles with physical captivity: she is restrained while men beat her; she is held in jail; she is even tied down in the hospital. Zach, too, is a character of captivity and liberation. Like Rosaleen, he is put in jail. But his bigger struggle is to break free of societal mores and become an attorney.

Lily and Forgiveness

As the mystery of Deborah Fontanel Owens unfolds, Lily's feelings surrounding her mother undergo a radical transformation. Lily's initial response to memories of her mother is a need for forgiveness and absolution: "That night I lay in bed and thought about dying and going to be with my mother in paradise. I would meet her saying, 'Mother, forgive. Please forgive,' and she would kiss my skin till it grew chapped and tell me I was not to blame. She would tell me this for the first ten thousand years."

Lily undergoes a roller coaster of emotions. The guilt and longing shift to denial and anger at the thought that Deborah would have left her. When Lily's fears are confirmed, her feelings shift to hatred. But when Lily learns that her mother married T. Ray because she was pregnant, the old guilt re-emerges. Then, when Lily learns how much Deborah loved her newborn baby, she falls again back into the old pit of longing. Part of Lily's struggle with her mother is figuring out what to believe: Did her mother want her or not? Did she love Lily, or did she abandon Lily to an inadequate father?

While Lily begins needing forgiveness *from* her mother, she eventually finds she needs to offer forgiveness *to* her mother. She recognizes the difficulty of this: "People, in general, would rather die than forgive. It's *that* hard. If God said in plain language, 'I'm giving you a choice, forgive or die,' a lot of people would go ahead and order their coffin." . . .

Even though forgiveness is something we do "to" other people, the real recipient of forgiveness is ourselves. Refusal to forgive is a burden that we—not the other person—must bear. Even at her young age, Lily recognizes this: "In a weird way I must have loved my little collection of hurts and wounds. They provided me with some real nice sympathy, with the feeling I was exceptional. I was the girl abandoned by her mother. I was the girl who kneeled on grits. What a special case I was."

As the novel concludes, Lily recognizes the plethora of "mothers" she has. Just as Jesus redefined family by making all followers his siblings, and making his biological mother the mother of the beloved disciple, Lily learns to redefine family. The mothers she now has include those who love her, guide her, teach her, and nurture her. . . .

The Queen Bee

The Secret Lives of Bees . . . is largely about community. Lily leaves her place of isolation out on a peach farm to find the warm communal embrace of the calendar sisters and the Daughters of Mary. Rosaleen, who lived by herself, finds refuge and companionship in the Boatwright household. May, who on her own would have been doomed to life in an institution, is affirmed and given purpose in the company of her sisters and friends. . . .

In *The Secret Life of Bees*, we learn that the role of a queen bee within a hive of worker bees is crucial. Without a queen, a group of bees becomes "completely demoralized" and die off. If the hive is not tended to carefully and the queen has no place to lay her eggs, there is a risk of a swarm. The queen bee's role is to lay the eggs: She is the mother of every bee in the hive. As such, she must be tended, not only by human caretakers, but by a group of attendant bees who groom and comfort her so that she can do her job. There must be a queen, but there can only be one.

In the Boatwright household, each woman plays a role in its smooth operation. In turn the household revolves around each of the women in a particular way: May's bent toward unquenchable sorrow is accommodated; the family tiptoes around June's relationship issues. The calendar sisters hover around Rosaleen, tending her wounds. When Lily faints or reflects on and adjusts to the news of her mother, the sisters hold her with care and tenderness. Within the community, each woman takes center stage as her need demands.

But the person orchestrating the entire household and its functioning is the eldest of the calendar sisters: August. We will consider August as the "queen bee" in the novel. She coordinates not only the household but also the honey operation and religious life. She offers guidance in everyday life as well. Like the queen of a beehive, August acts as mother in many ways to those who find their way to the bright pink house. She is most often the main "actor" in crisis situations, and she keeps the family history. . . .

Queen in Community

Gradually Lily comes to feel integrated into her new community. A key turning point in her awareness happens after May's death, when Sugar-Girl references the foolishness of the drive-by window at the white funeral home. Her comment sends the Daughters of Mary into hysterical laughter.

> But I will tell you this secret thing, which not one of them saw, not even August, the thing that brought me the most cause for gladness. It was how Sugar-Girl said what she did, like I was truly one of them. Not one person in the room said, *Sugar-Girl*, really, *talking about white people like that and we have a white person present*. They didn't even think of me being different.

In this caring community, Lily flourishes. Her skinny figure begins to fill out. Her skills and interests are encouraged. Her personality is not threatened or squelched, but embraced and loved. Her spiritual and ethical life is tended to.

As the Daughters of Mary celebrate Mary Day, they rub honey into the statue. The movement of their hands forms a stirring metaphor for community:

> Our lady was covered with hands, every shade of brown and black, going in their own directions, but then the strangest thing started happening. Gradually all our hands fell into the same movement, sliding up and down the statue in long, slow strokes, then chansons to a sideways motion, like a flock of birds that shifts direction in the sky at the same moment, and you're left wondering who gave the order.

Most people are part of more than one community, and sometimes loyalties can conflict. When Zach and Lily drive into town on an errand, they come upon a standoff between a group of young black men and a group of older white men. When one of the black men throws a bottle that hits one of the white men, Lily desperately wants Zach to reveal the culprit rather than go to jail with the group. But Zach keeps quiet. As Lily interprets it, "He chose to stand there and be one of them."

Over the course of *The Secret Life of Bees*, the Boatwright household gradually envelops Lily. Lily's adoption into the

Daughters of Mary and into the Boatwright home may challenge our notions of what constitutes community. Although she is a white girl among older black women, she eventually feels accepted. . . .

Beyond Expectations

Like many of the women in the Bible, women in *The Secret Life of Bees* act as individuals, not always following what family or society might expect, especially in matters of the heart. Each of the major characters bucks expectations according to what she believes to be best for herself. August, for example, refuses to consider marriage, seeing it as another potential "restriction" on her life.

Lily breaks "the rules" when she runs away from home, and then confounds even herself when she discovers her attraction to Zach. She confesses she had thought it would be impossible for a white girl to be attracted to a black man. "He had broad shoulders and a narrow waist and short-cropped hair like most of the Negro boys wore, but it was his face I couldn't help staring at. If he was shocked over me being white, I was shocked over him being handsome."

The two begin as friends, but their gentle teasing turns to flirting. Lily finds herself fantasizing about him, despite the many reasons why such a relationship would be impossible; "maybe desire kicked in when it pleased without noticing the rules we lived and died by."

Lily undergoes the usual stages of young love: roller-coaster emotions, vague anger, frustration, and unrelenting preoccupation. Unlike many smitten teenage girls, however, Lily never doubts her own worthiness. Many girls who become attracted to boys simultaneously begin to scrutinize themselves unfavorably. A girl might believe she is too fat, too smart, too ugly, too prudish. Lily, however, never questions her own adequacy in light of Zach.

Perhaps that is because the relationship is based on friendship with mutual encouragement. As Lily grows more attracted to Zach, she becomes more engrossed in her writing. Importantly, she also develops an appreciation for her body. Studying it in the mirror, she reflects: "It was the first time I'd felt like more than a scraggly girl." . . .

Following Her Own Heart

While *The Secret Life of Bees* gives us positive examples of male-female relationships, Kidd also makes it clear that women should claim their right to make decisions and act for themselves, even within a married relationship. For when a woman bows to societal expectations against her better judgment, she is bound to be unhappy, at best. At worst, and even against her intentions, her unhappiness will spread to her household, causing bitterness, anger, and resentment. . . .

Bucking the system is difficult. Through the experience of Deborah Fontanel Owens, we learn what can happen when a woman simply goes along with expectations despite misgivings. Most of the main characters in *The Secret Life of Bees* find fulfillment when they refuse to play by the rules culture has set for them. In the end the novel gives us hope that as our society changes, "rules" that prevent people from realizing their full potential as human beings can be abandoned or changed. As Lily receives her first kiss from Zach, she wells up with a sense of optimism as she anticipates transformation: "Changes were coming, even to South Carolina—you could practically smell them in the air." The immediate hope is for the cause of eradicating racism, but in a broader sense, it is a hope that oppressive structures of all sorts will be abandoned or transformed.

The Secret Life of Bees
Traces the Growth of Lily's
Social Consciousness

The Globe and Mail

The Globe and Mail *is a Toronto-based Canadian newspaper.*

The following review from the Globe and Mail *identifies the major themes of* The Secret Life of Bees *as mother-daughter relationships, the importance of community, and the power of forgiveness. During the course of the book, it states, Lily matures from a self-absorbed adolescent who is unquestioning of the racism surrounding her to a young woman committed to positive social change.*

Set in 1964 South Carolina, just after President Lyndon Johnson signed the Civil Rights Act, [*The Secret Life of Bees*] explores mother-daughter relationships, the importance of community and the power of forgiveness. In a gripping first-person narration that never falters, 14-year-old Lily Owens struggles to live with the possibility that, as a toddler, she found a loaded gun and accidentally shot her mother. Someone did, and Lily's father, T-Ray, who seems to care more for the family dog than for anyone else, cannot be trusted to reveal the truth. Fortunately for Lily, she is primarily raised by a loving field worker named Rosaleen Daise.

Rosaleen, who is black, is confronted by a group of racists one day while trying to register to vote. She spits tobacco onto one of the men's shoes and then, refusing to apologize, is brutally beaten and arrested, and both she and Lily are jailed. T-Ray retrieves Lily from prison but leaves Rosaleen to her own defence. After learning that the men in town plan to kill Rosaleen, and being told something shocking about her dead mother, Lily breaks Rosaleen out of jail and together they escape to Tiburon, a town whose name is written on the back of a Black Madonna Honey label once belonging to Lily's mother. There, they are taken in by the Calendar sisters—August, June and May Boatwright—who tend an apiary. Among the bees and a spiritual community of black women, Lily comes to realize that, as difficult as it may be living with a question, living with the answer may prove harder.

Motherhood and Love in a Difficult Time

Despite its weighty themes, the novel has enough humour to keep you reading, and [Sue Monk] Kidd has an enviable facility with dialogue, conveying lilting, drawling language which practically drips off the page to a musical rhythm. In fact, songs and music play a key role in the characters' lives. "A sound rushed up. A perfect hum, high-pitched and swollen, like someone had put the teakettle on and it had come to a boil . . . that's the sound of one hundred thousand bee wings fanning the air. You would have to hear it yourself to believe the perfect pitch, the harmony parts, how the volume rolled up and down." Also, Kidd's symbolic and metaphoric use of the Black Mary, or Black Madonna, as a stand-in mother for Lily, and a homemade wailing wall built for May, who has trouble distinguishing between others' suffering and her own, work beautifully to mine the nuanced themes of this book. Even the bees themselves evoke the spiritual and the maternal in a delightful way.

The sole disappointment in this otherwise imaginative read is the underdevelopment of Rosaleen, who begins as a full-blown character, but who fades quickly into the background, seeming to exist only in the service of Lily. Kidd is deliberate in showing racism operating between the girl and her caretaker on some level, indeed Rosaleen confronts Lily:

"I'm supposed to follow you like a pet dog. You act like you're my keeper. Like I'm some dumb nigger you gonna save." But for the remainder of the book, Rosaleen serves merely to absorb Lily's pain "like a sponge" and facilitate her story line, but is given little agency or depth. Clearly, Lily is set up as the hero of this tale—a dubious distinction in a novel about liberation of soul and self where August Boatwright and Rosaleen Daise provide two unflinching examples of freedom.

Nevertheless, *The Secret Life of Bees* does a good job of detailing Lily's internal shift, from an adolescent steeped in racism to a young woman who recognizes her prejudices and acts for positive social change. And it offers a unique vision of motherhood and love.

The Secret Life of Bees, much like Canadian writer Gail Anderson-Dargatz's *A Recipe for Bees*, is richly descriptive and enthralling, particularly as it relates to bee lore. This novel, with its southern American setting, its focus on adolescent and female relationships and its musicality, seems part *Fried Green Tomatoes* [film based on the Fannie Flagg novel *Fried Green Tomatoes at the Whistle Stop Cafe*], part *Are You There God, It's Me Margaret* [by Judy Blume], and, oddly enough, part "Flight of the Bumble-Bee" [orchestral interlude in Nikolai Rimsky-Korsakov's opera *The Tale of Tsar Saltan*]. Well worth the read.

Lily's Development Comes at the Expense of the Black Characters' Individualism

Linda Iraggi Larsen

Linda Iraggi Larsen is a multimedia studio artist. She was a student at the University of North Carolina–Asheville when this piece was written.

The African American characters in The Secret Life of Bees *are too good to be true, argues Larsen in the following selection, and thus are an example of the strain of racism that author Toni Morrison has identified in American literature. Although the novel is set during a time when life as a black person in the South was perilous, the realities of racism are merely glossed over, Larsen contends, with Sue Monk Kidd placing emphasis on the coming of age experiences of her young white protagonist.*

Set in 1964 against the backdrop of the rural South and the passing of the Civil Rights Act, white author Sue Monk Kidd's [2002] coming-of-age novel, *The Secret Life of Bees,* plays host to a number of extraordinarily positive African-American characters. After my reading of [novelist and critic] Toni Morrison's *Playing in the Dark: Whiteness and the Literary Imagination,* however, Kidd's characters no longer seem believable. Rather, these better-than-good portrayals of African-Americans, more readily become an example of the 'Africanist' presence of which Morrison speaks in her critical discussion of the ways in which the African-American presence has fashioned the American literary landscape. In *Playing in the Dark,* Morrison points out the use of the black presence in the narrative works of famed, canonized authors and exposes the metaphorical referents of race as a "division far more threatening to the body politic than biological 'race' ever was." Morrison uses six major "linguistic strategies employed in fiction to engage the serious consequences of blacks," to guide the reader in identifying and reexamining literary characterizations of African-Americans and the contexts in which they appear. By applying these linguistic strategies to a close reading of *The Secret Life of Bees* I will consider one of Morrison's thoughtful questions, "How do embedded assumptions of racial (not racist) language work in the literary enterprise that hopes and sometimes claims to be 'humanistic'?" . . .

Morrison Identifies Forms of Racism

Originally delivered as part of Harvard's William E. Massey, Sr. Lecture Series, Toni Morrison's treatise on American literary criticism, *Playing in the Dark: Whiteness and the Literary Imagination* focuses on what she terms the "Africanist" presence and how it has shaped the imagination and scholarship of American literature. Ensconced within the intellectual dominance of canonical literature, "American writers," says Morrison, "were able to employ an imagined Africanist persona to articulate and imaginatively act out the forbidden in American culture." Using examples of narratives by authors such as [Ernest] Hemingway, [Willa] Cather and [William] Faulkner, to name a few, Morrison's *Playing in the Dark* examines the fabrication of this Africanist persona by shifting "the [reader's] critical gaze from the racial *object* to the racial *subject*; from the described and imagined to the describers and the imaginers; [and] from the serving to the served." Morrison identifies six major linguistic strategies that perpetuate the displacement and disconnection of blacks, giving the reader a new lens of awareness through which to examine American literature and the ways in which it is "complicit in the fabrication of racism." Morrison's investigation was not intended to discredit the writings of these authors but rose rather out of concerns that such a framework for analysis was absent from literary scholarship [which was] therefore incomplete. It is with this attitude and through Morrison's lens that I offer an analysis of white author Sue Monk Kidd's contemporary novel, *The Secret Life of Bees*.

Reinforcing Racial Stereotypes

Set in the mid-sixties, just after the Civil Rights Act has passed, *The Secret Life of Bees* unfolds in rural South Carolina. Because the author chose to locate the story in the South, and to people it with multiple black characters to its one white protagonist (and several minor white antagonists), she provides ample evidence of the racialism that dominates American literature and has contributed to the classifying and stereotyping of individuals.

Despite what we know of the sixties as a time of intense struggle for change after a beleaguered history of racial violence, Kidd sets the novel in the distant past of softer times. The reader is tempted to luxuriate in idealizations of the white South—lazy, hot summers with an abundance of fresh food, simple comforts and picturesque settings—and dismiss the inequities that existed for black Americans. Safely segregated from the white world, African-Americans were either invisible or they were fodder for the romanticized myth of a happy-faced people, grateful and perfectly content in their place and position.

The story, narrated by a young white girl, reinforces such simplifications and uses the rising Civil Rights movement as a backdrop for the girl's personal quest for self-completeness and happiness. I am not certain whether to attribute the dismissive naiveté of the novel to the fourteen-year old narrator and protagonist, Lily Owens, or to the author. The complexities of living in the South as a black person during that time are glossed over. Though Monk sprinkles *The Secret Life of Bees* with episodic details that show some examples of racial conflict, their appearance has more to do with furthering the protagonist's journey than with deepening the dimensionality of the characters or locating the fictional landscape within an authentic period of history.

Missing from Kidd's romanticized novel are contributing factors that affect race, such as economics, class, women's issues, and differences between urban and rural settings, which leave her characters dislocated from a tangible, sociological framework. Had *The Secret Life of Bees* been written back in the sixties—the time in which it was set, rather than in 2002—it would be understandable, for at that time, public awareness of the disparity between the lives of blacks and whites in the South was suppressed. Attempts to keep racial inequities hidden from mainstream America were obvious to activists or to those connected to intellectual and socially aware communities but for the rest of white America, especially the North, the picture was that things weren't so bad. It might look that way on the news, but things just really weren't that bad, and would return to normal sooner or later. For writers who choose to take on black issues in American literature today, oversimplifying or omitting such contextual factors is untenable and presents a picture of the times in which discrimination seems to be "self-evidently valid and natural."

Kidd Objectifies Her Black Characters

Within this inauspicious landscape, Kidd predictably endows her protagonist, Lily, with unconditional entitlement to the minds and bodies of the black women characters while the black characters have neither the awareness of their objectification nor reciprocal entitlement. Morrison refers to this distancing as a way of reinforcing "a subordinate class from realms of value and esteem." For example, in the beginning of the book, Lily impassively introduces the reader to her house-keeper and nanny, Rosaleen, with an intimacy of physical detail that renders Rosaleen more as an object than as an individual.

> Rosaleen had worked for us since my mother died. My daddy
> ... pulled her out of the peach orchard, where she'd worked
> as one of his pickers. She had a big round face and a body
> that sloped out from her neck like a pup tent, and she was
> so black that night seemed to seep from her skin. She lived
> alone in a little house tucked back in the woods, not far
> from us, and came everyday to cook, clean, and be my
> stand-in mother. Rosaleen had never had a child herself, so
> for the last ten years I'd been her pet guinea pig.

Were Rosaleen a peripheral character, this physical description might suffice, but Rosaleen is a prominent character, and remains so, throughout the novel. With Lily presumptuously likening herself to Rosaleen's would-be, pet guinea pig, Kidd inadvertently presents Rosaleen as a voiceless projection of the white narrator's fancy. Just because Rosaleen is childless doesn't necessarily mean that she would choose the accommodating, care-giving, nanny/mammy role.

Early on in the novel Lily reveals (from an eight-year-old perspective) that she doesn't know Rosaleen's age because "she didn't possess a birth certificate." Rosaleen tells Lily that she is one of seven children and she "[doesn't] know where a one of [her siblings] is;" that in order to feed them all, her mother sold sweet-grass baskets on the roadside. Lily immediately dismisses Rosaleen's story and, without sympathy, launches into her own daydreams of ways in which Rosaleen could become her real mother or where "*she* [Rosaleen] could adopt *me*" [Lily] (emphasis added). Kidd inserts these few poignant details of Rosaleen's history but misses the opportunity of portraying Rosaleen as a character with an identity and a viewpoint of her own. Instead, Rosaleen is treated as a prop and serves the function of furthering the narrative.

Another example of Lily's one-way entitlement to intimacy is illustrated in the spaces between the conversation she is having with Rosaleen. Lily's emotionless description of Rosaleen begins, "Her lip was rolled out so far I could see the little sunrise of pink inside her mouth." While looking at Rosaleen who is shelling butter beans in preparation for Lily and her father's dinner, she continues, "Sweat glistened on the pearls of hair around her forehead. She pulled at the front of her dress, opening an airway along her bosom, big and soft as couch pillows." Lily's privilege and easy access to Rosaleen's body is not reciprocal and reinforces a conceptual separation of human beings through what Morrison describes as "metonyms [figures of speech in which the name of an object or concept is used to signify another related word of which it is a part] that displace rather than signify the Africanist character." Almost immediately following this voyeuristic [spying on the intimate behaviors of another] description of Rosaleen, Lily orders her to "Come look at this thing." Lily orders Rosaleen; she does not ask her. And finally Rosaleen is objectified even further with Lily's projection as normative and valid: "I was the one who knew that despite her sharp ways, [Rosaleen's] heart was tenderer than a flower skin and *she* loved *me* (emphasis added) beyond reason."

By chapter two, Kidd gives Lily the ability to leave her own space—her own body—and enter the mind of the black character altogether. Before, Lily had access only to Rosaleen's physical body; now, she is also capable of reading her thoughts and speaking for her. Overriding Rosaleen's ability to think and speak for herself, the author relays Rosaleen's feelings and thoughts through Lily's projection, as though it were Rosaleen's own voice. Rosaleen functions as a blank canvas for Lily's imagination. It is through Lily's white entitlement, not her increased intelligence, that Kidd unconsciously expands her white character's autonomy, and, in proportion, diminishes her black character. Kidd reveals her own disregard for the larger situation by neither exposing Lily's shallowness for what it is, nor ripening it into greater understanding and wisdom somewhere before the novel ends.

All About Lily

Kidd reinforces the inequities between the races with a heroic jailhouse/hospital break that Lily masterminds in order to save Rosaleen. "There is quite a lot of juice to be extracted from plummy reminiscences of 'individualism' and 'freedom,'" says Morrison, "if the tree upon which such fruit hangs is a black population forced to serve as freedom's polar opposite." Kidd moves the reader across the Southern landscape vacuously interrupting it from time to time with racially inspired dramas; but she does not deepen the reader's understanding of the racial complexities of the times. The main directive of the narrative remains Lily's search for the remnants of her mother's life. Although Kidd has constructed the relationship between Rosaleen and Lily based on mutual need, with Rosaleen as the escapee, she has little else to do but to assist Lily.

Eventually the two are led to the safe haven of the Boatwright sisters, a family of African American beekeepers who previously cared for Lily's mother prior to her death. From this point on, the story is tightly woven around the call-and-response theme of Lily's loss and search for her mother among these metaphorical, black mother figures. While Lily's pain at being motherless is justifiably deep and significant, the most significant attribute given the black characters—from Rosaleen to August Boatwright and her sisters—is their wide bosom for carrying pain, so much so, that it seems irrelevant if they should have a little more. Kidd records the tiniest details of the narrator's sentiments, from her fears to her pleasures, as poignant vicissitudes of life, pregnant with significance, while, in contrast, she blithely describes the black sisters as serenely steadfast, regardless of the greater challenges and hardships they have suffered. When Lily is finally ready to come to terms with her pain, it is August who bears it in another one-way interaction which Lily describes:

> I was pressed so close to her I felt her heart like a small throbbing pressure against my chest. Her hands rubbed my back. She didn't say, "Come on now stop your crying. Everything's going to be okay . . ." She said, "It hurts, I know it does. Let it out. Just let it out." So I did. With my mouth pressed against her dress, it seemed like I drew up my whole lifeload of pain and hurled it into her breast, heaved it with the force of my mouth, and she didn't flinch. She was wet with my crying. Up around her collar the cotton of her dress was plastered to her skin. I could see her darkness shining through the wet places. She was like a sponge, absorbing what I couldn't hold anymore.

The Boatwright's function in unison, as a selfless, idealized support system for Lily. As characters, they remain servile to the narrative, coming from nowhere and going nowhere on their own. For example, the particularly broad stroke Kidd uses to introduce and describe a local women's spiritual group, the Daughters of Mary, is so generalized the reader cannot distinguish one "daughter" from another. This illustrates what Morrison refers to as "economy of stereotype," another linguistic strategy that "serves primarily as a quick and easy image without the responsibility of specificity [or] accuracy." Beloved and behatted "Daughters" lend a dramatic Africanist presence to the novel's unfolding but they remain unknowable as individual characters outside the group identity.

Sue Monk Kidd's acknowledgments at the end of the novel, list five resource books about bees and insects. No list of resources relating to black identity or the contemporary African-American experience is mentioned. Perhaps this is why her portraits of African-Americans, though extremely likable, remain inauthentic—as imaginings not quite of this earth. Each and every one of the black characters is beyond reproach—models of integrity and moral excellence. But a fictional portrayal of an African-American character need not be better than good to be palpable, or recognizable as a positive Africanist presence.

Not Grounded in Reality

Kidd's use of a Black Madonna sculpture is central to the novel's theme. Through it, a distinctly Africanist presence permeates the air, epitomizing the mysterious *fetishization* [idol worship] to which Morrison alludes in *Playing in the Dark.* Kidd's Black Madonna, veiled in allegorical mystique, functions as the centerpiece for pulling the entire story into the universal theme of the Mother, the power of the feminine, and selfless love around which imaginative ceremonies play out. The problem with this Black Madonna is that it has no grounding in reality. Part Christianity and part homegrown myth, the Black Madonna springs from the author's imagination—a "dehistoricizing [depriving from historical context] allegory [that] produces foreclosure rather than disclosure." For example, where authentic African folklore establishes a cultural link to the Motherland and reinforces identity and pride for African-Americans, Sue Monk Kidd's Madonna reinforces the behaviors of slavery and oppression. In the fictionalized reenactment of "Our Lady of Chains," proclamations of freedom and overcoming are parodied but because the ritual is inauthentic the effects ring hollow. With this colorful and disjointed Madonna figure as the black community's symbol for hope, albeit, an empty, fabricated hope, both pride and meaning are displaced and diminished. "What is bound will be unbound. What is cast down will be lifted up. This is the promise of Our Lady;" yet the lasting image is of a black Madonna wrapped in chains. . . .

Applying [Morrison's] method of inquiry to *The Secret Life of Bees*, the novel becomes a case study of the ways in which the Africanist presence continues to survive in the contemporary literary landscape. By probing the questions about

Whiteness and the Literary Imagination from a subjective point of view, the reader's awareness of the limitations of a writer's capacity to create an authentic Africanist literary presence is expanded and deepened. Where knowledge remains disconnected from experiential reality, it has the tendency to fray into allegory and myth, or worse still, into idealizations that hold no great promise for moving us beyond a personal pathos to clear-sightedness.

Honey Child

Rosellen Brown

Rosellen Brown is an American author and instructor of English and creative writing. Her novels include Tender Mercies *and* Before and After, *which was made into a major motion picture.*

First-time novelist Sue Monk Kidd is to be commended for the elegance of her writing and her empathetic portrayal of a young girl's coming of age, writes Brown in the following article, but the novel suffers from a lack of reality. The serious issues of racism, accidental death, child abuse, suicide, and injustice are all addressed, but there is no real tension in the book, as the author leaves the clear impression that all will work out well in the end, Brown argues. As a result, she concludes, The Secret Life of Bees *has a fairy-tale quality that leaves something lacking for the adult reader.*

Anyone who reads a great deal of fiction—for the purposes of reviewing, teaching, contest judging, "blurbing"—will tell you that authority announces itself immediately. Though it's impossible to know on page one whether a writer possesses depth, consistency, or even seriousness of purpose, we can usually tell whether we're in good hands by the end of a few sentences.

Sue Monk Kidd's fine first novel *The Secret Life of Bees* begins with a paragraph in which she establishes the voice that will carry us pleasurably through her story, and lays out, implicitly, the emotional terrain she will take us through. The narrator is lying in bed listening to the bees that have squeezed through the cracks in her bedroom wall. She describes their

Rosellen Brown, "Honey Child," *Women's Review of Books*, vol. 19, no. 7, April 2002, p. 11.

sound, the glint of their wings, "and felt the longing build in my chest. The way those bees flew, not even looking for a flower, just flying for the feel of the wind, split my heart down its seam."

By the end of that paragraph we know a lot—short of her name and age—about Lily Owens. If we're paying attention, we take note of the demographics: bees at large in her bedroom, cruising in not via door or window but through less than solid walls. And, of course, we notice the attentiveness to detail of a sensitive, empathetic observer. Finally, unavoidably, we hear the desperate sadness of someone with modest emotional expectations—"not even looking for a flower"—that are not being met. This is solid writing, efficient, elegant and poignant.

It is 1964, in small-town Georgia peach country. Lily turns out to be the fourteen-year-old daughter of T. Ray, a man of implacable rage and vengefulness who in his bad moments, which are many, makes his daughter kneel on grits (a particularly Southern form of legal brutality). He mocks her, he beats her; his generally cruel behavior accounts for her envy of the freedom of honeybees. But, worse, the reason Lily has no one to stand between her and the tyranny of her father is that she herself, at the age of four, appears to have shot her mother accidentally when she picked up a gun in the course of a confrontation between her parents. Now, to turn the thumbscrews still tighter, T. Ray taunts his daughter by claiming that on the day of the shooting, her mother was about to flee and planned to leave her behind.

Abandoned twice over and accustomed to pain, it's no wonder that, in her futile attempts to conjure up her mother, Lily thinks, "Even her picking a switch off the forsythia bush and stinging my legs would have been welcome." Her mother, when they meet in heaven, will forgive her "for the first ten thousand years" and for the next ten thousand will fix Lily's hair, because "You can tell which girls lack mothers by the look of their hair."

The only care Lily has grown up with has been supplied by her black housekeeper, Rosaleen, who—in the tradition, pioneered by Dilsey [Gibson, of William Faulkner's *The Sound and the Fury*], of indispensable servants who don't cut their charges much slack—is a bracing combination of warmth and coolness, affection and correction. On the day of Lily's fourteenth birthday, which her father pointedly ignores, Lily and Rosaleen take a fateful walk into town so that Lily can buy herself a present and Rosaleen can register to vote.

So begin the complications, which become considerably tangled but emotionally simple: this is how two women, a female Huck and Jim [characters of Mark Twain's *Huckleberry Finn*], make a break for freedom and dignity. Like bees that seem to fly randomly, they will turn out to know exactly what they need and what will feed them.

Rosaleen, challenged, gets herself jailed for spitting on a white man's shoes, a provocation both brave and foolhardy; the feisty Lily springs her and, loosed from their assorted prisons, they take off. Lily is carrying one of her few mementoes of her mother, the "end-all mystery," a small wooden picture of a black Madonna on the back of which someone has written the words "Tiburon, N.C." There, not surprisingly, is where she heads, and there, aided by the kind of coincidence that under the circumstances is probably not as implausible as it seems, she encounters in the Tiburon general store the same strange painting of Mary on a bottle of locally made honey. As if to forestall scepticism, but quite in character, Lily insists that "there is nothing but mystery in the world, how it hides behind the fabric of our poor, browbeat days, shining brightly, and we don't even know it."

Suffice it to say, when Lily and Rosaleen follow their yellow brick road to the idiosyncratic compound of three black women bee-keepers, May, June and August, they come upon a trio that embodies every form of maternal nurturance and emotional education Lily needs, and a comfortable nest for

Rosaleen as well. In the Boatwright sisters, for whom the black Madonna is queen, Kidd has created a wonderful fantasy, a sort of beloved community, part Oz, part ashram, part center for racial reconciliation.

August, the oldest, is wise and patient, the kind of woman who knows every secret intuitively. May, the youngest, whose twin committed suicide years earlier, is now more sensitive than a tuning fork: whenever something disturbs her loving nature, she flees to her own private "wailing wall" to subdue her demons. The middle sister, June, gives Lily what appears to be the swat of a reverse racism that the humane, naive young girl, as white as her name, cannot understand. And there is a boy, Zach, black and beautiful, who (rather too un-selfconsciously for Georgia in 1964) dares, without notable angst, to love Lily. Flies (rather than bees) in the ointment also land him in jail and compromise the peace of the farm. But all is well in the end, every uncertainty settled as surely as if this were a detective story. Lily even sees her way to a hedged sympathy for her father, who, she realizes, lost a wife the day she lost a mother.

Both the strength and the weakness of *The Secret Life of Bees* are exemplified by the presence at the head of every chapter of brief excerpts from books such as *Man and Insects, The Queen Must Die: And Other Affairs of Bees and Men, Exploring the World of Social Insects, Bees of the World*. Glosses for what's to come, they raise the engaging and unanswerable question of whether we're like the bees or the bees are like us. But though the quotations are undeniably intriguing, their smooth fit with the story is a touch too perfect, as if to point out conveniently snug connections we must not be allowed to miss. Kidd must have found them irresistible.

But this is, they confirm, a novel in which everything meshes smoothly. Though it is never frivolous, there is in it the sweetness and trust that things will work out in the end that one tends to see in comedy, not tragedy; or perhaps, more appropriately, in the comfort of fairy tales that put their characters through harsh trials so that, every demon slain, they can triumph reassuringly over danger. At tale's end, the princess-scullery maid, the cast-out wanderer through the dark wood, will be saved, even cherished. For all the volatility of its subjects—violent death, child abuse both physical and emotional, suicide, racism and injustice—I had a hard time believing that anything truly terrible or irrevocable would be allowed to happen in these pages. There are no rough edges, no threat of unresolvable pain, though many atrocious things happen, or threaten to happen, along the way.

To be fair, whether that is cause for complaint or celebration will finally be a matter of taste. Lest this description seem to patronize an ingenious and generous book, let me add that Kidd scatters a good deal of wisdom like Hansel and Gretel's [from the Brothers Grimm German fairy tale "Hansel and Gretel"] redemptive bread crumbs en route to the consoling denouement. "It was foolish to think some things were beyond happening," Lily thinks, dreaming about the flawless Zach, "even being attracted to Negroes. I'd honestly thought such a thing couldn't happen, the way water could not run uphill or salt could not taste sweet. A law of nature . . . You gotta imagine what's never been, Zach had said." Taken in that spirit, the world Kidd has imagined has the force of homespun myth.

Lily finds a good many of these perceptive, confiding discoveries planted along the road to a reconciliation not only with herself but with her history and her future; they make her endearing and her story a satisfying blend of salty sweetness. But there are those—clearly I vacillated—who will also find its lovingkindness like honey, nourishing but a touch cloying. Curmudgeonly, perhaps, but unless a book is meant for the very young we resist comfort that comes too readily. A consoling balm, *The Secret Life of Bees* has less sting in the end than its swarm of griefs would seem to promise.

Solving Mysteries Leads to Spiritual Growth in *The Secret Life of Bees*

Charles Brower

Charles Brower is an editor and writer.

Mysteries are central to The Secret Life of Bees, *maintains Brower in the following selection. There are several types of mysteries in the novel, he suggests: supernatural mysteries, the secrets that the characters keep from each other, the secrets of nature, and the mysteries of the human heart. As Lily unravels these mysteries, she undergoes a spiritual awakening, Brower explains, and gains self-awareness and serenity.*

As suggested even in its title, the driving forces behind the characters' actions in Sue Monk Kidd's *The Secret Life of Bees* are mysteries. They may be mysteries that characters cherish—as with the kind represented by the supernatural events of the story of Our Lady of Chains recited ritually by her worshippers, the Daughters of Mary—or ones that they want desperately to resolve, as with Lily Owens's pursuit of answers about her mother's life and death. Characters keep secrets even from those they love, and nature seems to withhold its secrets from all except those who know how to look for them.

The Mysteries of the Human Heart

Lily's relationship with her mother, Deborah, whom Lily accidentally shot and killed when she was four years old, exists only in the imagination of the now fourteen-year-old teen-

Charles Brower, "Critical Essay on *The Secret Life of Bees*," in *Literary Newsmakers for Students*, vol. 1, ed. Anne Marie Hacht. Detroit: Gale, 2006, pp. 232–50. Copyright © 2006 by The Gale Group. All rights reserved. Reproduced by permission.

ager. Her abusive father, T. Ray, does not discuss his dead wife. Other than her memories of the day of Deborah's death, Lily has only a few mementos of her mother—a photograph, a pair of white gloves, and, most significantly, an icon of a dark-skinned Virgin Mary—which she keeps buried in her father's peach orchard. She digs them up occasionally and uses them to spin elaborate fantasies about the sort of woman Deborah was. The significance of the Black Madonna icon is a complete mystery to Lily, and the inscription on the back in her mother's hand, "Tiburon, S.C.," is what draws her to that small Southern town and the Boatwright sisters.

Lily learns who the Black Madonna is almost immediately upon arriving in Tiburon, but this knowledge only involves her in greater mysteries. The figure of Mary that August Boatwright and her sisters call Our Lady of Chains was originally a masthead, washed up, according to their legend, from an unknown ship near a plantation on the South Carolina coast in the days of slavery. It communicated in secret with the slaves of the plantation, exhorting them to furtive acts of flight and resistance. Amazingly, under its own power it repeatedly escaped the chains the plantation owner used to lock it in the barn. Shrouded in myth, Our Lady of Chains comes to represent, over the course of the novel, the mysteries Kidd portrays as the most powerful of all: those of the human heart.

Secrets Abound

The person who initiates Lily into these mysteries is August, beekeeper and apparent leader of the Daughters of Mary. As Lily keeps secrets from August—the truth about her life and especially the reason she has come to Tiburon—so August keeps from Lily the fact that she recognized her almost immediately from her resemblance to her mother, for whose family she served as housekeeper when Deborah was a child. Only when Lily is willing to be honest with August—and, more importantly, with herself—does August tell her about her mother.

An 1891 engraved illustration of a peach tree by Jules Trousset. Lily keeps the few mementos she has from her mother safe by burying them in her father's peach orchard.

Mysteries, indeed, are a vital part of life to August. As a beekeeper, she appreciates that the life of the hive is mostly hidden within the wooden bee boxes she has spread throughout the area. Taking Lily on as a sort of apprentice, she explains to her the inner workings of the hive, "the secret life we don't know anything about." Lily imagines that she loves "the idea of bees having a secret life, just like the one I was living," but her glimpse at this hidden life seems to have an overwhelming effect on her. Lost in a cloud of bees after August opens a bee box, Lily drifts into a trance in which her anguish about the "motherless place" within her is soothed by the queen bee, "the mother of thousands," as August tells her. Other secret aspects of nature are cherished by August, for whom the advances of scientific knowledge can also mean "the end of something." After watching a news report about the imminent launch of the unmanned rocket *Ranger 7* to the moon, August remarks:

> [A]s long as people have been on this earth, the moon has been a mystery to us. Think about it. She is strong enough to pull the oceans, and when she dies away, she always comes back again. My mama used to tell me Our Lady lived on the moon and that I should dance when her face was bright and hibernate when it was dark. . . . Now it won't ever be the same, not after they've landed up there and walked around on her. She'll be just one more big science project.

As August's mother's story suggests, the mysteries of nature and those of the Black Madonna are inextricably intertwined. The origins of the story of Our Lady of Chains that the Daughters of Mary listen to August recite on their annual celebration of "Mary Day" (the Feast of the Assumption [August 15]) are unclear. August says of their worship of Our Lady of Chains that she and her sisters "take our mother's Catholicism and mix in our own ingredients." August learned the story from her grandmother, as it had been passed along through generations along with the black wooden statue. The Daughters become entranced when August tells the story, chanting at the climactic, supernatural explanation of the statue's name—and as she does later when surrounded by bees, Lily is overwhelmed by the experience and faints.

Lily Learns to Forgive

The emotional, religious, and nature themes of *The Secret Life of Bees* all appropriately come to a climax around the same point of the novel. Having been prevented from talking to August by her and June's period of mourning after sister May's suicide, Lily finds the courage finally to come clean during the Daughters' celebration of Mary Day, when the story of Our Lady's unsuccessful imprisonment is reenacted, the black statue wrapped in chains overnight and then anointed in honey the next day. Lily has to share her sleeping space in the honey house with the chained effigy the night after learning that her mother had abandoned Lily, at least temporarily, to her father; she lashes out violently, shattering the glass jars stored there, seething with anger over her mother's betrayal:

> I felt a powerful sadness, not because of what I'd done, as bad as that was, but because everything seemed emptied out—the feelings I'd had for her, the things I'd believed, all those stories about her I'd lived off of like they were food and water and air. Because I was the girl she'd left behind. That's what it came down to.

With her worst fears about Deborah confirmed, Lily looks even more desperately to Our Lady and to August to fill the motherless place within her. As she is the keeper of the secrets of life inside her beehives, so August seems to be, more than any of the other Daughters, keeper to the secrets of Our Lady of Chains. Thus, the most important lesson she has to teach Lily about Mary is that the nurturing power of her divine motherhood—to Lily she is, like the queen bee, "mother to thousands"—is actually located within:

> You don't have to put your hand on Mary's heart to get strength and consolation and rescue, and all the other things we need to get through life.... You can place it right here on your own heart. *Your own heart.*

Lily's recognition of this symbolic importance of the Mary statue enables her to begin to forgive herself for killing her mother, as well as forgiving her mother for abandoning her (an abandonment that became permanent when Deborah came back to collect Lily and, in the ensuing scuffle with her enraged husband, was accidentally shot by her daughter). Even so, in this healing process there is the acceptance of mystery:

> Drifting off to sleep, I thought about her. How nobody is perfect. How you just have to close your eyes and breathe out and let the puzzle of the human heart be what it is.

Lily's spiritual development to some extent mirrors Kidd's own embrace of a feminist spirituality, as described in her 1996 spiritual memoir *The Dance of the Dissident Daughter*, the book that she wrote immediately preceding beginning work on *The Secret Life of Bees*. Kidd was a practicing Southern Baptist for most of the first forty years of her life but had a spiritual awakening that led her to reconnect with her feminine soul, as she terms it—"a woman's inner repository of the Divine Feminine." Lily is nominally a Baptist in Kidd's novel, but the leader of her Baptist church, Brother Gerald, is mean and cowardly. As Lily has her own spiritual awakening, she finds nourishment in the mysteries of Our Lady and the secrets of nature, as opposed to the tyranny of white authority, represented by corrupt police, an un-Christian minister, and her abusive father. Thus the novel ends with an abundance of mothering for Lily, with her summer of discovery turning into an "autumn of wonders." Lily's last line of the novel—"They are the moons shining over me"—explicitly calls to mind her and August's conversation earlier in the novel about the mysteries of the moon and the Virgin Mary's presence in it. With the acceptance of mystery comes a measure of serenity in Lily's life.

CHAPTER 3

Social Issues
in Literature

Contemporary
Perspectives on
Coming of Age

The Teenage Brain Is Wired to Tackle New Challenges

Nancy Shute

Nancy Shute, president of the National Association of Science Writers, covers science for National Public Radio, blogs for www.usnews.com, and is a contributor to National Geographic, Scientific American, and other publications.

During the past decade, scientists have learned that the brain is still a work in progress during adolescence, with the prefrontal cortex, which is responsible for impulse control and judgment, not fully mature until the early twenties, Shute reports in the following article. This explains why teenagers are prone to indulge in risky behaviors and often exhibit poor judgment, she states. Although the natural impulse of parents confronted with these facts of science is to be more protective of their teenagers, this can be counterproductive, Shute suggests. The teenage brain is uniquely able to process new information, which means that the teenage years are the best time to tackle new challenges.

Behold the American teenager, a lump in a hoodie who's capable of little more than playing *Grand Theft Auto*, raiding the liquor cabinet, and denting the minivan, thanks to a brain so unformed that it's more like a kindergartner's than a grown-up's. That's the message that seemed to emerge from the past decade's neuroscientific discoveries: that the brain, once thought to be virtually complete by age 6, is very much a work in progress during adolescence and not to be trusted.

But experts now are realizing that the popular parental response—to coddle teens in an attempt to shield them from every harm—actually may be counterproductive.

Not Fully Formed Until Adulthood

Yes, teenagers make woefully errant decisions that factor big in the 13,000 adolescent deaths each year. And yes, their unfinished brains appear to be uniquely vulnerable to substance abuse and addiction. But they also are capable of feats of learning and daring marvelous enough to make a grown-up weep with jealousy. How they exercise these capabilities, it now appears, helps shape the brain wiring they'll have as adults. "You have this power you're given," says Wilkie Wilson, codirector of DukeLEARN, a new program at Duke University designed to teach teenagers how to best deploy their brains. Far from coddling the kids, he says, Mom and Dad need to figure out how to allow enough "good" risk-taking to promote growth and prevent wasted talent—while also avoiding disaster.

It can be a nerve-racking exercise. "These kids are such a crazy mix of impulsiveness and shrewdness," says Marcia Harrington, a survey researcher in Silver Spring, Md. She recalls the time she thought her then 16-year-old daughter, Alexandra Plante, had sleepover plans, but the girl instead ditched school and flew to Chicago to visit an acquaintance she'd met briefly during a family trip. The scheme was revealed only because bad weather delayed the flight home. Alex returned unharmed and has never conceded that the escapade was too risky. "She's going to be a great adult someday," says Harrington. "But, boy, there are moments that are terrifying." Further along the road to adulthood now, Alex has applied her daring spirit to becoming an emergency medical technician and volunteer for the local fire department, and to heading off to college 2,500 miles from home.

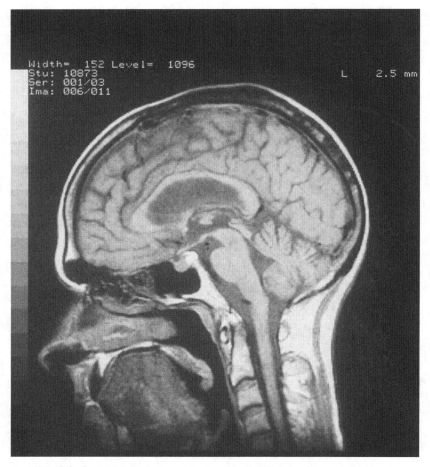

An MRI of the brain. Magnetic resonance imaging (MRI) technology reveals that the prefrontal cortex, responsible for impulse control and judgment, is not fully developed until after age twenty. © Mira/Alamy.

Still pruning. While society has known since forever that adolescents can be impulsive risk-takers, it wasn't until the 1990s, when MRI [magnetic resonance imaging] scans became a common research tool, that scientists could peek into the teenage cranium and begin to sort out why. What they found astonished them. The brain's gray matter, which forms the bulk of its structure and processing capacity, grows gradually throughout childhood, peaks around age 12, and then furiously "prunes" underused neurons. By scanning hundreds of children as they've grown up, neuroscientists at the National Institute of Mental Health [NIMH] have been able to show that the pruning starts at the back of the brain and moves forward during adolescence. Regions that control sensory and motor skills mature first, becoming more specialized and efficient. The prefrontal cortex, responsible for judgment and impulse control, matures last. Indeed, the prefrontal cortex isn't "done" until the early 20s—and sometimes even later in men.

Meantime, the brain's white matter, which acts as the cabling connecting brain parts, becomes thicker and better able to transmit signals quickly. Recent research shows that this myelination process of white matter continues well past adolescence, perhaps even into middle age.

Wired to Take More Risks

Now, dozens of researchers are studying how all these changes might affect adolescent behavior, and also shape adult skills and behavior, for good and for ill. The maturation lag between emotional and cognitive brain centers may help explain why teenagers get so easily upset when parents see no reason, for example; teens seem to process input differently than do adults. In one experiment, young teenagers trying to read the emotions on people's faces used parts of the brain designed to quickly recognize fear and alarm; adults used the more rational prefrontal cortex. Deborah Yurgelun-Todd, the researcher at McLean Hospital in Belmont, Mass., who led this work, believes young teens are prone to read emotion into their interactions and miss content. Therefore, parents may have better luck communicating with middle-schoolers if they avoid raising their voice (easier said than done) and instead explain how they're feeling.

Other experiments shed light on why even book-smart teenagers come up short on judgment: Their brain parts aren't talking to each other. When Monique Ernst, a child psychiatrist and neurophysiologist at NIMH, uses functional MRI to watch teenage and adult brains engaged in playing a gambling game, she finds that the "reward" center lights up more in teens than in adults when players are winning, and the "avoidance" region is less activated in teens when they're losing. There's also less activity in teens' prefrontal cortex, which adults use to mediate the "yes!" and "no" impulses from other brain regions. "The hypothesis is that there is this triumvirate of brain regions that needs to be in balance" in order to produce wise judgments, says Ernst, whether that's to wear a seat belt or use contraception.

Adult guidance. There is as yet no proven link between bright blobs on an MRI and real-life behavior, but researchers are hard at work trying to make that connection. In a 2005 study by Laurence Steinberg, a developmental psychologist at Temple University, teenagers in a simulated driving test were twice as likely to drive dangerously if they had two friends with them—and brain scans showed that the reward centers lit up more if teens were told that friends were watching.

A savvy parent might conclude that what's needed in the teen years is more guidance, not less. In fact, study after study has shown that one of the most powerful factors in preventing teenage pregnancy, crime, drug and alcohol abuse, and other seriously bad outcomes is remarkably simple: time with responsible adults. "It doesn't have to be parents, necessarily," says Valerie Reyna, a professor of psychology at Cornell University. But it does mean that teenagers are directly monitored by someone responsible so they have less chance to get in trouble. Reyna thinks adults also need to teach what she calls "gist" thinking, or the ability to quickly grasp the bottom line. Instead, she says, teenagers often overthink but miss the mark. When Reyna asks adults if they'd play Russian roulette for $1 million, they almost universally say no. Half of teenagers say yes. "They'll tell you with a straight face that there's a whole lot of money, and they're probably not going to die. It's very logical on one level, but on another level, it's completely insane."

If it's any comfort, the evidence suggests that teenagers' loopy behavior and combativeness is hard-wired to push them out of the nest. Adolescent primates, rodents, and birds also hang out with their peers and fight with their parents, notes B.J. Casey, a teen brain researcher who directs the Sackler Institute at Weill Medical College of Cornell University in New York City. "You need to take risks to leave your family and village and find a mate."

Built to Learn

The revved-up adolescent brain is also built to learn, the new research shows—and those teen experiences are crucial. Neurons, like muscles, operate on a "use it or lose it" basis; a teenager who studies piano three hours a day will end up with different brain wiring than someone who spends that same time shooting hoops or playing video games. A 16-year-old who learns to treat his girlfriend with care and compassion may well develop different emotional brain triggers than one who's thinking just about the sex.

Only in early childhood, it turns out, are people as receptive to new information as they are in adolescence. The human brain is designed to pay attention to things that are new and different, a process called salience. Add in the fact that emotion and passion also heighten attention and tamp down fear, and teenagerhood turns out to be the perfect time to master new challenges. "You are the owners of a very special stage of your brain development," Frances Jensen, a neurologist at Children's Hospital Boston, tells teenagers in her "Teen Brain 101" lectures at local high schools. "You can do things now that will set you up later in life with an enhanced skill set. Don't waste this opportunity." (She was motivated to create the talks by her own befuddling experiences as a single mother of two teenage boys.)

Jordan Dickey is one teen who seized opportunity. As a 14-year-old high-school freshman, he asked his father for something unusual: a $26,000 loan to start a business. The Dickey family, of Ramer, Tenn., raised a few cattle, and Jordan had noticed that people paid a lot more for hay in square bales than for the same amount in less-convenient round bales. After doing a feasibility study as an agriculture class project, Jordan convinced his dad to give him a three-year loan to buy a rebaling machine. He worked nights and week-ends, mowing, raking, and rebaling; paid friends $7 an hour to load the bales into a trailer; and hired drivers to deliver the hay to local feed marts, since he was too young to drive. "It taught me how to manage my own money," Jordan says.

That's an understatement. Not only did he pay off the loan in one year, he made an additional $40,000. Now 17 and a senior, he has saved enough money to pay for a big chunk of college, much to his parents' delight. "He likes for the job to get done and get done right," says Perry Dickey, who owns an electroplating shop. "It was a big responsibility for him, and I'm glad he took the lines and produced."

At Risk for Addiction

Teens can apply the new findings to learn more without more study, notes Wilson, whose DukeLEARN program will be tested in ninth-grade health classes next year [2009–2010]. Key points:

- Brains need plenty of sleep because they consolidate memory during slumber.
- The brain's an energy hog and needs a consistent diet of healthful food to function well.
- Drugs and alcohol harm short- and long-term memory.

Teens' predisposition to learn has a bearing on the vexing issue of teenage drinking, smoking, and drug use. Neuroscientists have learned that addiction uses the same molecular pathways that are used in learning, most notably those involving the neurotransmitter dopamine. Repeated substance use permanently reshapes those pathways, researchers say. In fact, they now look at addiction as a form of learning: Adolescent rats are far more likely to become hooked than adults.

And epidemiological studies in humans suggest that the earlier someone starts using, the more likely he or she is to end up with big problems. Last month [January 2009], a study tracking more than 1,000 people in New Zealand from age 3 to age 32 found that those who started drinking or using drugs regularly before age 15 were far more likely to fail in school, be convicted of a crime, or have substance abuse problems as an adult. "You can really screw up your brain at this point," says Jensen. "You're more vulnerable than you think."

A "safe" age? The new brain science has been used as a weapon by both sides of the drinking-age debate, though there is no definitive evidence for a "safe" age. "To say that 21 is based on the science of brain development is simply untrue," says John McCardell, president of Choose Responsibility, which advocates lowering the drinking age to 18. But there's also no scientific basis for choosing 18. The bottom line for now, most experts agree: Later is better.

Jay Giedd, an NIMH neuroscientist who pioneered the early MRI research on teen brains, is fond of saying that "what's important is the journey." Researchers caution that they can't prove links between brain parts and behavior, or that tackling adult-size challenges will turn teenagers into better adults. But common sense suggests that Nature had a reason to give adolescents strong bodies, impulsive natures, and curious, flexible minds. "Our generation is ready for more," insists Alex Harris, 20, of Gresham, Ore., who, with his twin brother, Brett, writes a blog and has published a book urging teens to push themselves. Its title: "Do Hard Things."

Society Will Benefit If Young People Assume Responsibility at an Earlier Age

Newt Gingrich

A former Speaker of the US House of Representatives, Newt Gingrich is a Republican politician, author, and political consultant.

There is ample evidence that adolescence has failed as a social institution in the United States, Gingrich argues in the following article. To support his claim, he cites rampant drug use and the prevalence of sexually transmitted diseases in teenagers as well as the lack of global competitiveness of American teenagers in the areas of math and science. Adolescence should be replaced with young adulthood, Gingrich contends, with young people being exposed to a shorter but more intense and focused educational period that makes them productive members of society at an earlier age.

It's time to declare the end of adolescence. As a social institution, it's been a failure. The proof is all around us: 19% of eighth graders, 36% of tenth graders, and 47% of twelfth graders say they have used illegal drugs, according to a study by the National Institute on Drug Abuse and the University of Michigan. One of every four girls has a sexually transmitted disease, suggests a recent study for the Centers for Disease Control. A methamphetamine epidemic among the young is destroying lives, families, and communities. And American students are learning at a frighteningly slower rate than Chinese and Indian students.

The solution is dramatic and unavoidable: We have to end adolescence as a social experiment. We tried it. It failed. It's time to move on. Returning to an earlier, more successful model of children rapidly assuming the roles and responsibilities of adults would yield enormous benefit to society.

Prior to the 19th century, it's fair to say that adolescence did not exist. Instead, there was virtually universal acceptance that puberty marked the transition from childhood to young adulthood. Whether with the Bar Mitzvah and Bat Mitzvah ceremony of the Jewish faith or confirmation in the Catholic Church or any hundreds of rites of passage in societies around the planet, it was understood you were either a child or a young adult.

In the U.S., this principle of direct transition from the world of childhood play to the world of adult work was clearly established at the time of the Revolutionary War. Benjamin Franklin was an example of this kind of young adulthood. At age 13, Franklin finished school in Boston, was apprenticed to his brother, a printer and publisher, and moved immediately into adulthood.

John Quincy Adams attended Leiden University in Holland at 13 and at 14 was employed as secretary and interpreter by the American Ambassador to Russia. At 16 he was secretary to the U.S. delegation during the negotiations with Britain that ended the Revolution.

Daniel Boone got his first rifle at 12, was an expert hunter at 13, and at 15 made a yearlong trek through the wilderness to begin his career as America's most famous explorer. The list goes on and on.

It is true that life expectancy was shorter in those days and the need to get on with being an adult could be argued. Nevertheless, early adulthood, early responsibility, and early achievement were the norm before the institution of adolescence emerged as a system for delaying adulthood and trapping young people into wasting years of their lives. To regain

An eleven-year-old girl works in a textile mill in early twentieth-century Tennessee. Viewpoint author Newt Gingrich argues that today's adolescents should be engaged in real work. © Lewis W. Hine/George Eastman House/Getty Images.

those benefits, we must develop accelerated learning systems that peg the rate of academic progress to the student's pace and ability to absorb the material, making education more efficient.

Adolescence was invented in the 19th century to enable middle-class families to keep their children out of sweatshops. But it has degenerated into a process of enforced boredom and age segregation that has produced one of the most destructive social arrangements in human history: consigning 13-year-old males to learning from 15-year-old males.

Undermining Communities

The costs of this social experiment have been horrendous. For the poor who most need to make money, learn seriously, and accumulate resources, adolescence has helped crush their future. By trapping poor people in bad schools, with no work opportunities and no culture of responsibility, we have left them in poverty, in gangs, in drugs, and in irresponsible sexual activity. As a result, we have ruined several generations of poor people who might have made it if we had provided a different model of being young.

And for too many middle-class and wealthier young Americans, adolescence has been an excuse to delay work, family, and achievement—and thus contribute less to their own well-being and that of their communities.

It's time to change this—to shift to serious work, learning, and responsibility at age 13 instead of age 30. In other words, replace adolescence with young adulthood. But hastening that transition requires integrating learning into life and work. Fortunately, innovations in technology and in financial incentives to learn offer hope.

The Information Age makes it possible for young people to learn much faster than our current failed bureaucracies and obsolete curriculums permit. New systems such as Curriki, founded by Sun Microsystems and now an independent nonprofit, allow a community of teachers and learners to collaborate via the Internet to create quality educational materials for free—giving every American access to learning 24 hours a day.

And experiments such as the one my daughter, Jackie Cushman, is running in Atlanta—where poor children are paid the equivalent of working in a fast-food restaurant to study and do their homework—are examples of a more dynamic future.

In math and science learning, which are among the most important indicators of future prosperity and strength, America lags far behind such emerging powers as China and India. Studying to compete with Asian counterparts in the world market is going to keep U.S. teens busier than anyone ever imagined. This will require year-round learning, with mentors available online, rather than our traditional bureaucratic model of education. But we must go further, toward a dynamic, real-world blueprint for learning.

Indeed, going to school should be a money-making profession if you are good at it and work hard. That would revolutionize our poorest neighborhoods and boost our competitiveness.

The fact is, most young people want to be challenged and given real responsibility. They want to be treated like young men and women, not old children. So consider this simple proposal: High school students who can graduate a year early get the 12th year's cost of schooling as an automatic scholarship to any college or technical school they want to attend. If they graduate two years early, they get two years of scholarships. At no added cost to taxpayers, we would give students an incentive to study as hard as they can and maximize the speed at which they learn.

Once we decide to engage young people in real life, doing real work, earning real money, and thereby acquiring real responsibility, we can transform being young in America. And our nation will become more competitive in the process.

Some Adolescents Are Burdened by Bad Parents

Susan B. Miller

A clinical psychologist, Susan B. Miller is also the author of a novel, Indigo Rose, *and books on psychology, including* Disgust: The Gatekeeper Emotion.

All parents have problems to deal with, but some parents have major, lasting issues that make them poor parents some of the time, maintains Miller in the following selection. Although teenagers may be tempted to ignore the problem, the best way to cope with a poor parent is to face the truth, Miller counsels. There are several ways to recognize a problem parent, she states. Problem parents include those who ignore the needs of their children, fail to take a reasonable amount of responsibility for their children, or pressure their children to become someone they are not, Miller explains.

Troubled parents are not all the same. Some parents are abusive or neglectful; their kids may find them cruel or uncaring. Some parents suffer a great deal because of a mental illness or a painful loss or a difficult set of experiences they've not been able to overcome; their children may pity them and feel helpless about their suffering. Other parents have dangerous habits such as drug or alcohol abuse, shoplifting or gambling; or they do distressing things such as carrying on extramarital affairs. You wish they'd stop what they're doing, but they don't, no matter how much they hurt the people around them. Though troubled parents come in many forms, they present some shared challenges and difficulties for their children. . . .

Susan B. Miller, "Chapter 1: Getting Started," in *When Parents Have Problems: A Book for Teens and Older Children Who Have a Disturbed or Difficult Parent.* Springfield, IL: Charles C. Thomas, 2012, pp. 3–9. Copyright © 2012 by Charles C. Thomas Publisher, Ltd. All rights reserved. Reproduced by permission.

Face the Truth

Thinking about parents' problems isn't pleasant. Many kids work hard to believe their parents have no serious problems, even when the evidence points in the other direction. You may love your parents very much, or want to love them, and feel it's not right to think of them as troubled. But, unless you're an ostrich, it's best not to stick your head in the sand. Seeing what's true—even if that truth isn't pretty—helps you to cope better with the real situation you're in. Seeing an unpleasant truth is never a reason to feel guilty. Recognizing what's there doesn't make you disloyal or unkind; it doesn't mean you're trying to hurt or shame your parent. You're not creating the problem; you're just seeing it, which is better than closing your eyes and your mind.

Another approach kids may take to their parents' problems is to try to live as if their parents mean nothing at all to them and as if they need no parents. That's an understandable strategy if your parent causes you pain and difficulty, but it has its limitations. All kids need parenting. Nature made us that way. We grow up gradually, over many years, and we need a great deal of help along the way. . . .

Parents Can Have a Variety of Problems

Sometimes a parent's problems show up most clearly as behaviors a child wishes the parent would stop, but the parent doesn't stop. For example, your mother drinks too much and gets nasty or sexually inappropriate when she's drinking. Or your father gambles and wastes the family's money so there's not enough for rent, school expenses or good food. Or maybe your father or mother has affairs, making for lots of tension between the two adults on whom you rely. Often they seem to hate each other and you may wish (but fear) that they would just divorce. Or your mother uses drugs and may be spaced-out or doing irresponsible, frightening things like feeding your baby sister food that's not good for her or driving recklessly; maybe she gets arrested or she makes you angry by lying in bed all day.

Parents' problems can come in other forms as well. Some parents are always unhappy and they complain to their children about how miserable they are. Kids worry that their mother or father might go on feeling sad forever or might commit suicide. Some parents feel very anxious and jittery, or they can't go out of the house without getting panicky. And some parents have a mental illness so they can't function at all normally; they have odd experiences, like hallucinations, that their kids don't understand; or they talk a mile a minute about crazy-sounding things and stay up all night; or they're convinced against all reason that the neighbors are trying to poison them. A mentally ill parent may have too much on his mind or too much wrong with his mind to take care of you. He may neglect you entirely, or confuse your needs with his own or your brother's, or he may attend to you but give you bad advice that's due to his mixed-up thinking. For example, a paranoid parent may tell you to wear a disguise if you have to go to the neighbor's to borrow the lawn mower, or to watch out for the woman that lives in the green house because she's trying to kill your family or to listen in on your thoughts. Or a manic parent may insist you go out shopping with him at four in the morning. Or he might want to spend hours showing you sexy pictures on the Internet and think that's incredibly funny and fun but then snap at you if you're not amused.

Some troubled parents have no obvious illness, but yet something is . . . wrong with them. They may get along poorly with other adults. Maybe your mother gets into arguments and is rude to people so that you feel nervous and embarrassed when you're out in public with her. She may blow up at a waitress over some tiny thing or insult your schoolteacher. Some parents show their problems by being over-critical of others. They may get down on everyone around them; or they may pick one child or adult on whom to harp, for no good reason; they may pick one person to fault today, and someone else tomorrow. Other troubled parents may be overprotective and overanxious, or they may be huge perfectionists who are unable to relax or let you relax. They're nice enough but you don't feel very good around them.

Ignoring Their Children's Needs

You may feel confused about whether the problems you experience at home are yours or your parent's. That distinction can be hard to make, especially because both you and your parent may be making a contribution. Nevertheless, it can be valuable to try to sort it out, especially if you are the kind of person who tends to take blame for everything that goes wrong.

Let me give you a few guidelines that can help you get a better perspective on whether you have a troubled parent. These guidelines focus less on extreme behaviors (such as drug abuse or physical mistreatment) than on how your parent feels about you and acts toward you. They concern the relationship between you and your parent. I'll start with the idea that all people, whatever their age, have their own unique feelings and thoughts and their own needs and wishes. Each person has the right to expect that his feelings, thoughts, needs, and wishes will be treated with respect and taken into consideration by the people around him, especially by the adults who are there to care for him. Having your feelings and needs respected and considered does not mean that you'll always get what you want or that your needs will be put above everyone else's. It does mean that your parents will have an interest in knowing what your feelings and needs are and that they will not ignore or ridicule them.

One clear sign that a parent has serious problems is when the parent cannot look at the needs and wishes, feelings and thoughts of his or her child. The "not looking" may take a variety of forms. The parent may be too preoccupied with himself or caught up in the symptoms of his mental illness or addiction to notice or care. Or she may resent that her child's needs and feelings are different from her own so she ridicules the child. Or he may pay close attention to the child but come up with a very distorted view of the child's inner self, so that the child does not even recognize herself in the picture her parent paints. Or a parent may be attentive to the child some of the time but then become completely inattentive, perhaps because she is drinking too much, traveling all the time, going through a depression, or because she only pays attention to her child when he's doing something that meets her needs. Let me give an example of a troubled parent who is attentive to her child but paints a distorted picture of him that disregards his real feelings and needs:

> George is thirteen. His two best friends are going to summer camp for three weeks. George tells his mother he'd like to go to camp too. His mother's response is, "Wouldn't you be scared, George? You've never been away from home before." George says he's scared, but he wants to go. His friends are going and they're excited about it. He feels excited too, thinking of the fun he could have. His mother says she doesn't think George should go. He'll be too homesick and unhappy. He's not as adventurous as his friends and he's physically delicate. She tells him a story about her own bad experience at summer camp when she was thirteen. She details how lonely she was, how awful the food was and how the counselors were mean. George gets angry. "I'm not like you," he says. "I want to go to camp. I'm not delicate and I will have fun. You don't want me to have a good time," he yells. His mother gets furious. "Don't talk to me like that," she says. "I'm just trying to protect you. You've never been to camp before—I have. You've got a lot of nerve yelling at me when I'm looking out for your best interests. You talk big about camp now but wait till you get there and you're all alone." George feels confused, guilty, and dejected. And

worse yet, he now feels very afraid to go to camp because he doesn't think his mom will support him.

George's mother is a troubled parent who appears to be looking at her child's feelings and needs, but actually she isn't. She probably believes she's being helpful to George, but she's only looking at George's fear, because it's like her own fear, and she's ignoring his wishes for adventure and friendship and his wishes to grow up and be on his own. She paints a picture of George that isn't accurate, then she tries to force it on him, and she gets angry and offended when he won't accept it. She pushes him to feel guilty for rejecting her "concern," and she takes no responsibility for discouraging George's excitement and his adventurous spirit.

A Reasonable Amount of Responsibility

A troubled parent often has difficulty looking at her child and seeing what is inside that child. She also has difficulty looking inside *herself* and noticing her own feelings and behaviors. This second difficulty means that the parent will have a hard time taking a *reasonable amount* of responsibility for how her parenting affects her child. I say a reasonable amount of responsibility because some parents take too little responsibility for their children's feelings, some take too much responsibility, and some are confused and take responsibility when they're not responsible but fail to take responsibility when they are.

All these difficulties cause confusion for the child or teen, who is trying to sort out how his own feelings and behaviors are related to his parent's behavior. A parent who takes too little responsibility doesn't recognize when her child's anger, sadness or stubbornness is a response to neglect or abuse from the parent. The parent blames the child for having upset feelings, as if the feelings are just an annoyance to the parent and aren't the child's legitimate response to the home he's living in. George's mother is an example. She gets angry at

George for his complaints; she doesn't see that he has reason to complain about what she's done.

Parents who take too much responsibility also create problems for kids. If the child sneezes, the mom faults herself for not dressing the child properly. If the child gets a bad grade on a test he blew-off studying for, the dad feels responsible and gets depressed. Pretty soon the child feels trapped by his parent's excessive self-blaming. The child feels he has to be perfect (never get sick, never fail a test, and never feel sad) in order to protect the parent from worry. He may feel angry at his parent and then feel guilty for being angry at someone who worries so much about him. He may also get the feeling that nothing about him is his own, not even his problems. He has to share everything with his parent. He wants his own sneezes, his own bad grades, and of course his own good grades, too.

Some parents fault themselves at all the wrong times and leave their child confused about what reasonably can be expected from a parent. Such a parent may cruelly belittle a teenage son in public and not give that unkind behavior a thought, but then the parent apologizes to her son for not getting him an expensive computer for Christmas, when no apologies are needed. The child gets confused about his own importance. He feels very unimportant to his parent when that parent humiliates him without a thought; yet that same parent apologizes about not getting him a lavish gift, as if he were a prince who should have every single thing he wants and never a moment of frustration.

Another Sign of a Troubled Parent

One more sign of a troubled parent is that the parent needs the child to be a certain way, even when that way of being is not natural to that child. The parent constantly pressures the child to change and cannot love the child as she is. A parent may need her child to be a certain way in order to make up for failings the parent sees in herself. A parent may need a child to be thin or stylish or very successful in school or very accomplished as an athlete or musician. The parent is seldom satisfied with the child as she is and the child feels unloved.

Parents may have other kinds of strong needs regarding what their children should be. Though this sounds odd, some parents need their children to be failures or to be unattractive or to be stupid. Maybe the parent feels stupid and she doesn't want to be alone with that bad feeling, so she expects her daughter to be stupid with her, to make the parent feel less deficient and alone. If the daughter does well in school, the mother might get irritable or ignore the child or she might fill the child's time with household responsibilities so she can't study and continue to do well in school. This kind of parent is so controlled by her own strong need for the child to be this way or that way that she's not able to look at what's natural and good for the child.

If you still feel uncertain whether your parent has a serious problem that's making for difficulty between the two of you, or making for difficulty in your own feelings, think about whether your parent pays attention to your thoughts and feelings, needs and wishes, and at least tries to get a pretty accurate view of those aspects of you. And think about whether your parent looks at his own behavior and how that behavior affects you. One last thing to look at is whether you can talk to your parent when you feel he's shortchanging you. Will he take an honest look at his own behavior if you ask him to? A healthy parent is willing to look at what he's doing and take responsibility when he's making mistakes. He won't fault himself for things you do or act as if you're a baby who's not responsible for his own actions. Neither will he blame you for everything and refuse to look at himself. He'll look honestly at himself and you both and do the best job he can figuring out who is doing what. The analysis he comes up with may not be exactly like your own, but it won't be totally different either. It will sound reasonable to you and you'll likely feel glad that you and your parent talked.

Teenagers Need Positive Parental Role Models

Claire Ellicott

Claire Ellicott is a journalist for the Daily Mail, *a British newspaper.*

A British survey reveals that teenagers without positive role models of their own gender fare much worse than their peer who have such models, Ellicott reports in the following selection. Teenage boys with no male role models are less likely to find and keep a job, more likely to abuse drugs, more likely to engage in criminal behavior, and more likely to be depressed, she writes. Similarly, she notes, teenage girls with no female role models are less likely to find and keep a job, more likely to abuse alcohol, and more likely to feel suicidal.

Young men with no male role models in their lives and women without a mother figure struggle to keep their lives on track, a hard-hitting report warns.

Teenagers with No Role Models Suffer

The Prince's Trust youth index, the largest survey of its kind, found that young people without a positive figure of the same gender are 67 per cent more likely to be unemployed than their counterparts.

They are also significantly more likely to stay unemployed for longer than their peers, the report suggests.

It found that young men with no male role model are 50 per cent more likely to abuse drugs and young females in the corresponding position are significantly more likely to drink to excess.

Young people who have no positive figure of the same gender are also statistically much more likely to feel suicidal than those who do.

In total, more than a third of youngsters—34 per cent—admitted to having felt suicidal at some point, but this figure rose to 42 per cent for those without positive figures in their lives.

Nearly one in five young men with no father figure or positive male influence said they used illegal drugs, compared to one in ten with a male role model. There was also a pronounced difference in terms of alcohol abuse between girls with no positive female influence in their lives (19 per cent) and girls with one (16 per cent).

Young men with no male role model to look up to were twice as likely to turn or consider turning to crime as a result of being unemployed.

The report, which was based on interviews with 2,170 16- to 25-year-olds, revealed that one in three young men and almost a quarter of young women have no positive figure to look up to. It found that this was likely to impact significantly on their mental well-being and their outlook on life.

The research suggests that young women who do not have a female role model in their lives are particularly affected, with 50 per cent saying they have felt suicidal.

One in four young people say they lack a sense of identity.

However, this increases to more than one in three for young men without a positive male influence.

These young men are also three times more likely to feel down or depressed all of the time and significantly more likely to admit that they cannot remember the last time they felt proud.

They are also significantly less likely to feel happy and confident than those with male role models, according to the figures.

A father listens to an MP3 player with his teenage son. Research shows that teenagers with positive same-gender role models are less likely to struggle with unemployment, drug abuse, and depression. © bikeriderlondon/Shutterstock.com.

The Prince's Trust report, which was carried out by YouGov, suggests young people without male role models are more than twice as likely to lack a sense of belonging.

It also warns that unemployed young people are suffering mental health problems such as panic attacks, self-loathing and depression because they are out of work.

Adults Can Have a Positive Impact

Martina Milburn, chief executive of The Prince's Trust, which helps disadvantaged young people into work, said: 'It is nothing less than a tragedy that so many young people feel they don't have a role model.

'We should not underestimate the impact a positive adult influence can have on a young person.

'At The Prince's Trust, we give vulnerable young people the support they may have lacked earlier in life, helping to build self-belief and, in turn, develop skills for work.'

With no father to look to as he grew up, Arfan Naseer fell into a life of drugs and gangs.

He even spent time in prison after becoming involved with the wrong crowd, impressed by their expensive cars and gangster lifestyle.

He believes that if he had had a father or male role model to look up to, he would have seen the error of his ways at a much earlier age.

Mr Naseer, now 29, said: 'All I saw was these older men driving around with their big cars and I'm ashamed to say that I looked up to them like they were special.' In 2003, at the age of 21, Mr Naseer was sent to jail for a drugs-related offence.

He said prison changed him and convinced him he needed to sort out his life.

'I had no male role models around when I was younger because I was an only child and my dad passed away when I was five.

'I needed a father in my life or perhaps even an older brother—to guide me as a young man. My mum tried to make sure that I never missed having a dad but I did feel left out. She couldn't be the male role model I needed.'

Unresolved Loss in Childhood Can Lead to Issues Later in Life

Gordon Carson

Gordon Carson is a writer and editor for Community Care *magazine.*

Traumatic experiences early in life that are left unresolved can have devastating effects later in life, Carson suggests in the following article. In particular, he reports, parents who suffer a loss or trauma as a child and who are unable to come to terms with that experience are more likely to neglect or abuse their children.

A deep-seated loss or trauma suffered by a parent or child that is unresolved can have specific implications—and present particular challenges—for social workers and the families they support.

David Shemmings, a specialist in attachment theories and professor of social work at the University of Kent, says parenting problems, such as neglect and child abuse, can occur when losses or trauma experienced by parents have not been resolved.

"'Unresolved' here has a very precise meaning," says Shemmings, who is also director of the Assessment of Disorganised Attachment and Maltreatment (Adam) project in London. "For example, it doesn't mean that the person cries at the thought of their loss. The term indicates post-traumatic stress disorder and/or dissociation."

Jim Walker, an independent social worker and psycho-therapist, says in a Community Care Inform guide to unresolved loss and trauma that a traumatic childhood in itself "is not predictive of maltreatment of children. What is predictive is if the adult has not been able to come to terms with their traumatic experiences".

The guide says a common reaction to unresolved trauma is parental dissociation, with parents "likely to neglect the emotional needs of their children and/or have difficulty in assessing risk in their partners".

Walker adds: "There is also a strong correlation between unresolved loss and trauma and disorganised attachment in children. 'Unresolved' parents tend to have children whose behaviour is disorganised."

Social workers need to be in a position to judge whether unresolved loss or trauma is a factor in parenting problems.

One way of identifying whether a person is harbouring an unresolved loss or trauma is the adult attachment interview, in which open-ended questions are asked about childhood relationships and experiences.

Meanwhile, Shemmings' Adam project has developed a Maltreatment Pathway Model that identifies three key predicators of maltreatment from parental behaviour, one of which is unresolved loss and trauma.

Unresolved Loss

This model formed part of a training course he delivered to Croydon Council social workers in south London this year [2011].

The course also highlighted the relevance of unresolved loss to the wider children's services sector, particularly those working with young people who may have experienced severely traumatic events in their home countries before travelling to the UK [United Kingdom].

Katherine MacLeod, a social worker in Croydon's unaccompanied minors team, attended the course. MacLeod, who has just completed her first 18 months of practice after joining Croydon when she qualified, says the Adam training has "given me the tools to identify unresolved loss".

She says the issue of unresolved loss and trauma might be explored as part of core assessments of unaccompanied young people.

Shemmings says that talking with an "empathetic, non-judgemental listener goes an awful long way to helping" people showing signs of unresolved loss or trauma if they aren't also mentally ill.

"Certainly the evidence from event-based tragedies, such as Hillsborough, the Zeebrugge ferry disaster and the Bradford football stadium fire, is that survivors needed to talk and that helps enormously," he says.

"But they need to be given the time to do it, and often they need to go over the same ground again and again. The worker can't rush this process."

Shemmings says it can be more difficult to help people if the loss or trauma occurred when they were very young, and if the trauma is "relationally based", such as child abuse or rape, rather than based on an event such as a car accident.

"The most important thing to emphasise is that practitioners need training in this field of work," he adds, "as people experiencing unresolved loss can start to 'relive' aspects of the trauma in the room with the worker.

"It is sights, sounds and smells that (unconsciously) remind a person of the trauma, but they are usually unaware of the connection.

"This is why, if there has been early loss and trauma which is unresolved, the presence of a baby or toddler can 'activate' the original loss, because the infant's vulnerability reminds the adult of their own."

Walker, in an interview for this article, says social workers "must be prepared to explore in depth any unresolved loss or trauma".

"It takes some courage to do it. You have to ask questions in detail and try to find ways to help people to talk. People can be frightened and anxious about talking about it.

"They might not volunteer information and it may only emerge over time if they feel social workers are trustworthy and resilient enough to take it on board."

Sample questions, says Walker, could be to ask parents to recall three happy and three sad memories from their childhood, or the most frightening thing that happened to them as a child.

"If you keep coming back to questions like that, people may give up more and more information," he adds. "But if you just ask them blandly once, you are not going to get the whole picture. You have to be prepared to keep plugging away. You also have to be sensitive and not just go barging in."

To illustrate his point, Walker cites a child protection assessment he was carrying out, and it was only at the end of the final session with a parent that she revealed she had been abused by her grandfather.

There will be cases, however, that require more in-depth expertise in dealing with post-traumatic stress disorder, and psychotherapy could be appropriate.

Behavioural Therapy

The National Institute for Health and Clinical Excellence (Nice) also recommends trauma-focused cognitive behavioural therapy or eye movement desensitisation and reprocessing as possible treatments.

Walker believes that, though understanding trauma and loss has been given greater priority in the past 20–30 years, particularly in relation to neuroscience and the functioning of the brain, there is still more that could be done to map its impact on child protection.

"I would think that in the majority of child protection cases where I'm assessing parents, there's a significant element of unresolved loss and trauma," he says.

"The area of addictions and trauma is important too; for a lot of people who abuse substances it's about self-medication against emotional distress. My guess is that unresolved loss and trauma would be a major factor in the addictions field too."

For Further Discussion

1. The historical backdrop in *The Secret Life of Bees* is the civil rights movement in the American South. How does Sue Monk Kidd treat the topic of racism in the book? Refer to the Chapter 1 viewpoints to formulate your answer.

2. Lily passes through several stages of spiritual and emotional growth in *The Secret Life of Bees*. What are some of these stages? Cite from Susan Andersen's essay.

3. In what ways is *The Secret Life of Bees* a classic coming of age novel? Refer to Amy Lignitz Harken's article.

4. What are some of the mysteries at the center of *The Secret Life of Bees*? Cite from the selection by Charles Brower.

5. Susan B. Miller offers advice for children with a problem parent. Lily's father, T-Ray, is an abusive parent who shows no love toward his daughter. Does Lily follow Miller's advice? Are there other things Lily could have done?

For Further Reading

Olive Ann Burns, *Cold Sassy Tree*, New York: Ticknor & Fields, 1984.

Kim Edwards, *The Memory Keeper's Daughter*, 2005.

Leif Enger, *Peace Like a River*, 2001.

Fannie Flagg, *Fried Green Tomatoes at the Whistle Stop Cafe*, 1987.

Beth Hoffman, *Saving CeeCee Honeycutt*, 2010.

Zora Neale Hurston, *Their Eyes Were Watching God*, 1937.

Joshilyn Jackson, *Between, Georgia*, 2007.

———, *Gods in Alabama*, 2005.

Sue Monk Kidd, *The Mermaid Chair*, 2005.

Harper Lee, *To Kill a Mockingbird*, 1960.

Alice Sebold, *The Lovely Bones*, 2002.

Kathryn Stockett, *The Help*, 2009.

Rebecca Wells, *Divine Secrets of the Ya-Ya Sisterhood*, 2004.

Bibliography

Books

Ean C.M. Begg	*The Cult of the Black Virgin*. New York: Penguin, 1997.
Marjie Bowker and Ingrid Ricks	*We Are Absolutely Not Okay: Fourteen Stories by Teenagers Who Are Picking Up the Pieces*. Edmonds, WA: Edmonds School District, 2012.
Judith A. Cohen, Anthony P. Mannarino, and Esther Deblinger	*Treating Trauma and Traumatic Grief in Children and Adolescents*. New York: Guilford Press, 2006.
Wilbur Cross	*Gullah Culture in America*. Westport, CT: Praeger, 2008.
Bruce J. Gevirtzman	*An Intimate Understanding of America's Teenagers: Shaking Hands with Aliens*. Westport, CT: Praeger, 2008.
Sherri Mabry Gordon	*Beyond Bruises: The Truth About Teens and Abuse*. Berkeley Heights, NJ: Enslow, 2009.
Elizabeth A. Johnson	*She Who Is: The Mystery of God in Feminist Theological Discourse*. New York: Crossroad, 1992.
Malka Margalit	*Lonely Children and Adolescents: Self-Perceptions, Social Exclusion, and Hope*. New York: Springer, 2010.

Judith G. Smetana   *Adolescents, Families, and Social Development: How Teens Construct Their Worlds.* Malden, MA: Wiley-Blackwell, 2011.

Linda Tate   *A Southern Weave of Women: Fiction of the Contemporary South.* Athens: University of Georgia Press, 1994.

Periodicals

Laura J. Bloxham   "Review of *The Secret Life of Bees,*" *Dialog: A Journal of Theology,* Summer 2005.

Lucinda Dyer   "Sue Monk Kidd: *The Secret Life of Bees,*" *Publishers Weekly,* August 6, 2001.

Cheryl Easley   "Coming of Age in the 21st Century," *Nation's Health,* February 2009.

Judith Hebb   "Religious Imagery in *The Secret Life of Bees* and *The Mermaid Chair,*" Popular Culture Association/American Culture Association Conference, April 14, 2006.

Beth Kephart   "*The Secret Life of Bees.* (Review & Opinion: Sweet as Honey)," *Book,* January–February 2002.

Sue Monk Kidd and Cindy Crosby   "*PW* Talks with Sue Monk Kidd: Remembering the Spirit," *Publishers Weekly,* July 10, 2006.

Gerald Nachman   "The Teening of America: It Used to Be We Couldn't Wait to Grow Up. Now We Strive for Permanent Adolescence," *American Spectator*, December 2011.

Grace O'Connell   "Youth Revolt: The Refreshing Literary World of Post-apocalyptic Nightmares," *This Magazine*, May–June 2012.

Carl E. Pickhardt   "Rebel with a Cause: Rebellion in Adolescence," *Psychology Today*, December 6, 2009.

Rachel Simhon   "Honey Is the Balm," *Daily Telegraph* (London), February 23, 2002.

Tampa Tribune   "The Resonance of *Bees*," November 1, 2008.

USA Today (magazine)   "Increased Stress Puts More at Risk," April 2012.

Women's Health Weekly   "Stopping Adolescent Problems Progressing to Adulthood: Adolescents, Parents, and Governments Must Embrace Proven Prevention Programs," May 10, 2012.

Jeff Zaleski   "Review of *The Secret Life of Bees*," *Publishers Weekly*, November 12, 2001.

Jarrod Zickefoose   "Alternate Worlds, Past Passions in These Coming-of-Age Stories," *Cleveland Plain Dealer*, February 17, 2001.

Index

A

Adams, John Quincy, 97
Addiction, 94–95, 119
Adolescence, as failed experiment, 96–100
Adolescent brains, 88–95
The Adventures of Huckleberry Finn (Twain), 9
African American characters, 20, 64–65, 66–75
Africanist presence, in literature, 66–68, 71, 74–75
Andersen, Susan, 32–39
Anderson, Sherry Ruth, 49
Anderson-Dargatz, Gail, 65
August (*Secret Life of Bees*)
    Lily and, 33, 35, 42, 44, 49–50, 73, 82–83
    as mother figure, 55, 57, 79
    and Our Lady of Chains, 84, 85
    as queen bee, 59
    refusal to marry by, 61
    secrets of, 82–84

B

Bees/beekeeping, 37, 44–46, 55, 59, 76–77, 83
Behavioral therapy, 118–119
Biedermann, Hans, 45
Bildungsroman, 9–10
Black Madonna
    as central to theme of novel, 10–11, 20, 24–25, 74, 82
    as female image of God, 35, 41–42, 49, 53
    as mother symbol, 40–51, 64, 74, 85

mystery of, 84
statue of, *43*
as symbol of liberation, 29, 37, 57, 82
Black Madonna Honey, 17, 29
The Bluest Eye (Morrison), 41
Boatwright sisters (*Secret Life of Bees*)
    as characters, 73, 78–79
    community of, 53, 60–61, 64
    and Daughters of Mary, 10
    refuge taken with, 17, 24, 29, 42, 56, 58–59, 72
    See also specific sisters
Boone, Daniel, 97
Brain development, in adolescence, 88–95
Brower, Charles, 81–86
Brown, Rosellen, 76–80
Bruteau, Beatrice, 47

C

Calendar sisters. *See* Boatwright sisters
Captivity, 57
Carson, Gordon, 115–119
Casey, B.J., 93
The Catcher in the Rye (Salinger), 9
Catholic Church, 46
Childhood losses, 115–119
Chodorow, Nancy, 44
Christianity, and racism, 46–47
Churches, 46–47
Civil Rights Act, 28–29, 42, 63, 66, 68
The Color Purple (Walker), 34
Coming-of-age novels, 9–10
Community, 53, 58–61, 63